Prima's Official Strategy Guide

Mark Cohen

Prima Games
A Division of Random House, Inc.

3000 Lava Ridge Court
Roseville, CA 95661
(800) 733-3000
www.primagames.com

Prima's Official Strategy Guide

The Prima Games logo is a registered trademark of Random House, Inc., registered in the United States and other countries. Primagames.com is a registered trademark of Random House, Inc., registered in the United States. Prima Games is a division of Random House, Inc.

Associate Project Manager: Christy L. Curtis
Senior Project Editor: Brooke N. Hall
Editorial Assistant: Tamar D. Foster

http://thesims.ea.com/

Please be advised that the ESRB rating icons, "EC", "K-A", "E", "T", "M", "AO" and "RP" are copyrighted works and certification marks owned by the Interactive Digital Software Association and the Entertainment Software Rating Board and may only be used with their permission and authority. Under no circumstances may the rating icons be self-applied or used in connection with any product that has not been rated by the ESRB. For information regarding whether a product has been rated by the ESRB, please call the ESRB at 1-800-771-3772 or visit www.esrb.org. For information regarding licensing issues, please call the IDSA at (212) 223-8936. Please note that ESRB ratings only apply to the content of the game itself and does NOT apply to the content of this book.

Important:
Prima Games has made every effort to determine that the information contained in this book is accurate. However, the publisher makes no warranty, either expressed or implied, as to the accuracy, effectiveness, or completeness of the material in this book; nor does the publisher assume liability for damages, either incidental or consequential, that may result from using the information in this book. The publisher cannot provide information regarding game play, hints and strategies, or problems with hardware or software. Questions should be directed to the support numbers provided by the game and device manufacturers in their documentation. Some game tricks require precise timing and may require repeated attempts before the desired result is achieved.

ISBN: 0-7615-4097-0
Library of Congress Catalog Card Number: 2002111425
Printed in the United States of America

02 03 04 05 BB 10 9 8 7 6 5 4 3 2 1

Introduction

With the arrival of family pets in *The Sims Unleashed*, bladder control takes on a new meaning, as you accept the challenges of housebreaking your new Dog and keeping the Cat's litter box clean. But pet ownership is fun, with tricks, raccoon fights, gopher patrols, pet shows, and attack training.

The Sims Unleashed has some bonuses as well, including five new careers, a gardening function, and the introduction of Community Lots, where your Sims shop, play, and mingle. You can also build your own business, with more than 125 new items in Buy and Build modes.

This guide covers all the new features of *The Sims Unleashed*, including a glossary of new objects, and step-by-step instructions for adopting, raising, and breeding family pets. After millions of copies sold, *The Sims* still attracts new converts every day, so we also cover the original game, with updated interaction tables and complete tutorials on all aspects of Sim life. So, whether you're a veteran or a newbie, everything you need to find happiness and fulfillment as a Sim is within these pages. Here is a summary of what you'll find in this guide.

Part I: *The Sims*

The first part takes you on a detailed tour through the original *The Sims* game. We explain how a Sim thinks, acts, and reacts in various situations; and we teach you how to select and blend your Sim's personality traits. We cover each of the eight Motives, the primal urges that drive all Sims, and show you how to manipulate your Sim's world to create happiness and contentment.

Sims are social creatures; this can be a blessing or a curse. We show you how and why a Sim interacts with others, and explain the benefits and pitfalls that accompany every short-term and long-term relationship. If marriage and children are in your Sim's future, you can find out what to expect when the blessed day arrives.

Sims spend simoleans at a staggering rate, so you must think about a successful career. We cover all the career paths, with extensive tables detailing salaries, work schedules, and promotion requirements.

After analyzing the Sim psyche from all directions, we shift our focus to the physical world, which consists of a home and its many objects. Our building tutorials take you through every step of the construction process, from putting up the framing to slapping on the final coat of paint. Our topics include walls, windows, doors, wall coverings, stairways, second stories, pools, and landscaping.

A Sim home is empty until you fill it with stuff, and we provide facts and statistics on every object you can buy, over 150 items in all. In addition to data and descriptions, we use detailed lists and tables to show how items relate to each other, and how some objects can alter the effectiveness of others.

Part 2: *The Sims Unleashed*

Your Sims will find seven new Community Lots in *The Sims Unleashed*. We begin the second part of our guide with an in-depth tour of each location, including:

* Gothic Quarter
* Lake Barrett
* McArthur Square
* Sim Quarter
* Pet Paradise
* Sim Central Park
* Custer's Market

Next, we feature Dogs and Cats, the first new interactive personalities since the original *The Sims*. Topics include:

* Pet motives
* Housebreaking
* Obedience training
* Commands and tricks
* Pet show competitions
* Hunting
* Getting rid of pests
* Breeding

If your Sims are too busy for Dogs and Cats, they can ease into pet ownership with alternative animals, including Birds, Fish, Turtles, and Iguanas. These creatures require care and attention, but not as much as Dogs and Cats. Along with animals, your Sims have five new career tracks—Fashion, Culinary, Animal Care, Circus, and Education. As you climb the corporate ladder, consult our tables for promotion requirements, salaries, and working hours.

Finally, we include a complete glossary of new *The Sims Unleashed* objects, grouped by game menu category, and including prices, Motive interactions, and special notes. The last chapter includes extensive interaction tables, covering Sims and their new animals.

There you have it, a desktop tribute to Sims and their pets. Adopt a cat to keep the gophers out of your garden, or assemble a pack of hounds to terrorize the Gothic Quarter. The choice is yours as *The Sims Unleashed* gives you free rein to encourage your animal side.

PART 1:

The Sims™

CHAPTER 1:
WHAT'S YOUR SIM SIGN?

Introduction

When you are charged with the solemn task of creating a Sim from scratch, you have 25 points to distribute over five traits: Neat, Outgoing, Active, Playful, and Nice. Whether we admit it or not, all of us have an inherent wish to be perfectly balanced people (or Sims). Of course, you can take the easy way out and award five points in every category, creating a generic Sim. You'll spend less time managing a middle-of-the-road Sim because in most situations, he or she will do the right thing. If you'd rather play it safe, skip this chapter and move right to "Motives: I Want…I Need…Therefore, I Am a Sim". If not, read on as we describe the subtle (and sometimes dramatic) outcomes that your personality ratings will inspire.

It's in the Stars

As you play with the personality bars, you'll note the changing zodiac sign that appears on the screen. Of course, a serious astrologer would argue that a true personality profile is based on much more than five traits. However, if you have a basic understanding of newspaper horoscopes, you'll be able to recognize yourself, or someone close to you, as you create a Sim personality. In the next section we'll look at each trait and examine the potential effects of your ratings in various game situations. But first, let's take a look at basic interpersonal compatibility as seen through the eyes of the zodiac. The following table gives you the best and worst matchups for friends and lovers. This doesn't necessarily imply that any other Relationship outside of the table is doomed; it is merely an indication of how hard you'll have to work on it.

Sims Zodiac Compatibility Table

SIGN	ATTRACTED TO	REPELLED BY
Aries	Gemini/Taurus	Cancer/Libra
Taurus	Aries/Libra	Virgo/Cancer
Gemini	Pisces/Virgo	Capricorn/Aries
Cancer	Taurus/Scorpio	Gemini/Aries
Virgo	Aquarius/Sagittarius	Leo/Taurus
Libra	Virgo/Cancer	Pisces/Scorpio
Scorpio	Pisces/Leo	Libra/Aquarius
Sagittarius	Pisces/Capricorn	Libra/Scorpio
Leo	Sagittarius/Cancer	Capricorn/Gemini
Capricorn	Aquarius/Taurus	Leo/Gemini
Aquarius	Capricorn/Sagittarius	Scorpio/Virgo
Pisces	Scorpio/Gemini	Leo/Aries

Personality Traits

The following sections review what you can expect from each type of Sim, with examples of how different personality traits will manifest during the game. For our purposes, we'll divide the ratings bar into three sections: Low (1–3), Average (4–7), and High (8–10). These numbers correspond to the number of light blue bars to the right of each trait.

Neat

Low

Don't expect these Sims to pick up their dirty dishes, wash their hands after using the bathroom, or take timely showers. They are perfectly content to let others clean up their messes.

Fig. 1-1. The kitchen floor is a perfect place for this messy Sim's snack leavings.

Fig. 1-3. This fastidious Sim goes straight to the bathtub after a hard day's work.

Medium

At least these Sims keep themselves relatively clean, and you can depend on them to clean up their own messes. Occasionally they'll even clean up another Sim's garbage, but you might have to intervene if you have several cleanup items that need attention.

Outgoing

Low

Shy, reserved, Sims have less pressing needs for Social interaction, so it will be more difficult to pursue friendships with other Sims, although they can still carry on stimulating conversations. Within their own home, a shy Sim may be less interested in receiving hugs, kisses, and back rubs, so if you are looking for romance, it would be a good idea to find a compatible target (see zodiac chart on p. 2).

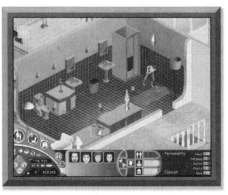

Fig. 1-2. After slopping water all over the bathroom during his shower, this moderately neat Sim mops up his mess before leaving the room.

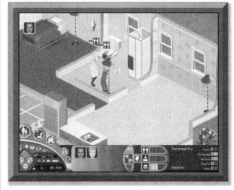

Fig. 1-4. This Sim cringes at the thought of a back rub—poor guy.

High

A super-neat Sim always checks the vicinity for dirty dishes and old newspapers, and of course, personal hygiene is a big priority. One of these Sims can compensate for one or two slobs in a household.

Medium

It will be a little easier to get this Sim to mix with strangers and enjoy a little intimacy from his housemates. Don't expect a party animal, but you'll be able to entice your guests into most activities.

Fig. 1-5. Come on everyone, let's hit the pool!

High

This Sim needs plenty of Social stimulation to prevent his or her Social score from plummeting. You'll have no trouble throwing parties or breaking the ice with just about any personality type.

Fig. 1-6. This outgoing Sim is still unconscious from last night's pool party, and she has inspired the close friendship of another man. Hmmm.

Active

Low

Forget about pumping iron or swimming 100 laps at 5:00 a.m. These Sims prefer a soft easy chair to a hard workout. A sofa and a good TV are high on their priority list. In fact, if they don't get their daily ration of vegging, their Comfort scores will suffer.

Fig. 1-7. This Sim says "No way!" to a session on the exercise bench.

Medium

These Sims strike a good balance between relaxing and breaking a sweat. They dance, swim, and even shoot hoops without expressing discomfort.

Fig. 1-8. His Active rating is only a four, but that doesn't stop this Sim from shooting hoops in his jammies.

High

Active Sims like to pick up the pace rather than fall asleep on the sofa in front of the TV. Get these Sims a pool, basketball hoop, or exercise bench, and plan on dancing the night away with friends.

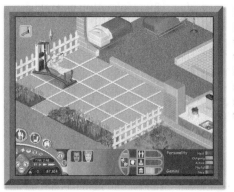

Fig. 1-9. Even in her business suit, this active Sim will gladly leave Mortimer on the sofa and pump some iron in the backyard.

Playful

Low

Get these Sims a bookcase, a comfortable chair, and plenty of books. If reading isn't an option, looking at a painting or playing a game of chess will do just fine.

Fig. 1-10. There's always time to watch the fish, for this less-than-playful Sim.

Medium

These well-rounded Sims are usually receptive to a good joke and don't mind a little tickling. They may not be the first ones on the dance floor, but they'll join in with a good crowd.

Fig. 1-11. This Sim is Playful enough to dance, even though she is overdue for a shower.

High

Can you spell P-A-R-T-Y? These Sims love to have a few drinks, dance to good music, and invite lots of guests over to the house. They love telling jokes, and they are usually ready to laugh at others' stories.

Fig. 1-12. This Playful kid would get the Maid in the pool for a game of chicken, if only she would respond.

Nice

Low

There is nothing redeeming about a grouchy Sim. They are always ready to tease or insult their friends, and they love to brag. A Sim with a low Nice rating should be dropped from your guest list immediately, or asked to leave if he or she shows up.

Fig. 1-13. Usually a compliment elicits a nice response, but not so with with sourpuss.

Medium

This Sim keeps an even keel about most things. Of all the traits, Nice is the least destructive if you award at least four points. Only the nastiest Sims can get under a medium-Nice Sim's skin.

Fig. 1-14. This Sim has time for a good tickle, even while mopping up the bathroom.

High

These Sims just want to make the world a better place for everyone. If there was a Sim beauty contest, the winner would be extremely "Nice."

Fig. 1-15. Even after spending the night on the kitchen floor, this Sim still knows how to compliment her mate.

Personality Tables

The following tables demonstrate how personality traits affect Fun scores and Skill development.

Traits that Raise Max Fun Value

PERSONALITY TRAIT	RAISES MAX FUN SCORE FOR
Playful	Aquarium, Chess Table, Computer, Doll House, Flamingo, Pinball, TV (Cartoon Channel), VR Glasses
Serious (Low Playful)	Newspaper (Read)
Active	Basketball Hoop, Play Structure, TV (Action Channel)
Outgoing	Hot Tub, TV (Romance Channel)
Grouchy (Low Nice)	TV (Horror Channel)

Skills Accelerated by Personality

SKILL	OBJECTS USED TO INCREASE SKILL	TRAIT ACCELERATOR
Creativity	Easel, Piano	Playful
Body	Exercise Machine, Swimming Pool	Active
Charisma	Medicine Cabinet, Mirrors	Outgoing

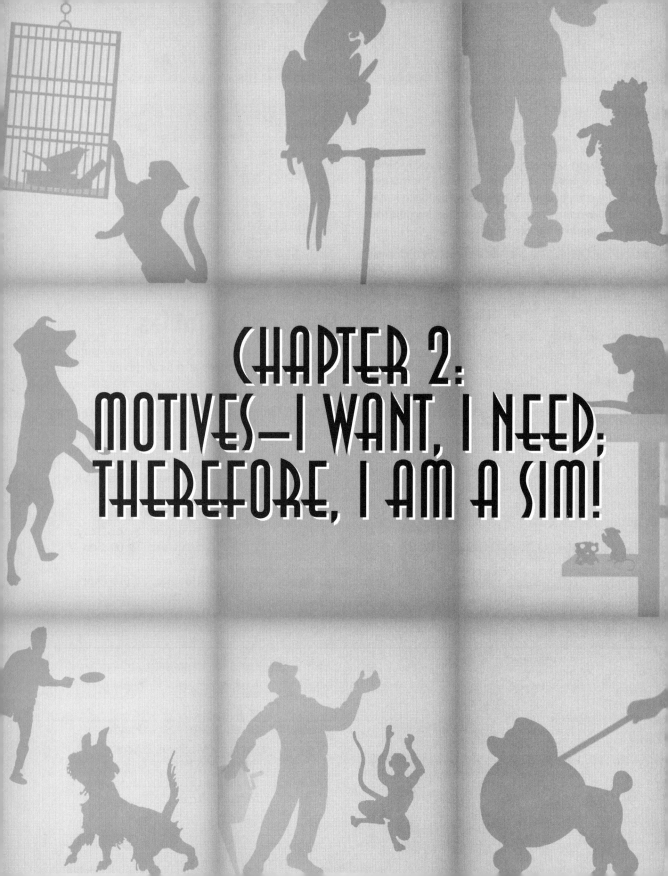

CHAPTER 2:
MOTIVES—I WANT, I NEED; THEREFORE, I AM A SIM!

Introduction

When you consider how many needs, traits, and desires make up a Sim's personality, it would be an injustice to call it AI. Never before has a computer-generated character interacted so completely with both the game and the gamer while maintaining a unique (and ever-changing) personality. Is it any wonder that *The Sims* has topped the PC sales chart for nearly two years running?

In the previous chapter we discussed a Sim's personality traits. It painted a broad picture of the various types of Sims you might encounter in the game, much the same as a newspaper horoscope tells a superficial story of a person's life. In this chapter, we advance from broad-brush personality traits to the eight powerful Motives that drive a Sim's every action. We cover each Motive in detail, but first, let's begin with a few basic definitions.

What Is a Motive?

A Motive is, very simply, a need. Your Sims follow these needs, based on their own instincts and a little help from you. If you activate Free Will in the Options menu, your Sims will also make their own decisions, based on changing needs. After selecting a Motive to fulfill, be it Hunger or Hygiene, the Sim is "rewarded" with Motive points. These points raise the corresponding Motive score.

The eight Motive scores are displayed on the right side of the control panel. A Motive rating is considered positive if the bar is green, and negative if it is red. Internally, the game uses a 200-point system, with positive (green) ratings between 0 and 100, and negative (red) ratings from 0 to -100.

> **TIP**
> When any of the Sims' eight Motives drop below a certain level, a Sim will cease an activity that doesn't improve the Motive in distress. So, you'll see low-priority items drop out of the activity queue, or your Sim will add an activity that addresses the critical need.

> **CAUTION**
> *Without Free Will, your Sims depend entirely on your input to keep them alive. If you don't tell them to eat, they will starve, and eventually die.*

Mood Rating

The game control panel also displays a Mood Rating, just to the right of the Sim character icons. If the rating is positive, you see up to five green bars displayed above the comedy/tragedy masks. When the Mood Rating is negative, it displays up to five red bars below the masks.

In calculating the Mood Rating, each of the eight Motives is weighted, based on how critical it is to sustaining a Sim's life. Hence, Hunger, Bladder, and Energy, which are all related to a Sim's physical well-being, carry more weight than the noncritical Motives such as Social, Fun, or Room. So, if a Sim is hungry and tired, as pictured in figure 2-1, the overall Mood Rating will be relatively low, even if several other Motives are high.

Fig. 2-1. This Sim kid's overall Mood Rating is barely positive, due to the fact that he is starving and low on Energy.

The Motives

In the following sections we describe the eight Motives, using several tables to show you how and why a Sim reacts to different objects in the environment. By recognizing the relationships between Motives and objects, you'll begin to understand how a Sim considers a perpetual barrage of options. Once you do this, the only remaining question is, "Who is really in charge here, you or the Sim?"

Fig. 2-2. This Sim family enjoys a meal together. Mom's Hunger bar is in the worst shape, so she has a second meal plate at the ready.

NOTE

Aside from the overall Motive weighting system, each Sim suffers different rates of Motive depreciation based on personality traits. For example, a Playful Sim must have more "rewards" to maintain the Fun Motive bar. Similarly, an Outgoing Sim requires more interaction with other Sims to maintain the Social score.

Hunger Score for Each Meal, Snack, or Gift

MEAL TYPE	HUNGER MOTIVE BAR POINTS
Snack	9
Quick Meal	16
Full Meal	16
Group Meal (per serving)	16
Pizza (per serving)	33
Candy Box (gift)	3 (per serving, 12 servings per box)
Fruitcake (gift)	7 (per slice, 6 slices per box)

Hunger

For obvious reasons, a Sim cannot survive for very long without food. We'll cover the details of food preparation in a later chapter, but for now let's focus on the basics. As long as you have a refrigerator, a Sim can enjoy a Snack, Quick Meal, Full Meal, or Group Meal (same as a Full Meal, except one of the Sims prepares several servings). In addition to preparing food, a Sim with a telephone can order out for Pizza, or enjoy food that was brought as a gift (Candy Box or Fruitcake). The Hunger Motive bar points awarded with each meal are outlined in the following table.

Comfort

The next category listed in the Needs section of the control panel is considerably less important than Hunger. Sims like to be comfortable, and they love cushy chairs, oversized sofas, and supportive beds. Spending more money on these objects translates into greater Motive rewards. However, if your budget is tight, you must still furnish the house with basic furniture or your Sims will express their discomfort.

Fig. 2-3. With only a cheap chair and loveseat, this Sim's Comfort score is mired in the red.

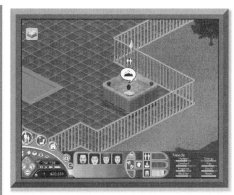

Fig. 2-4. Three out of four Motive scores are on the way up while this couple enjoys a hot tub soak.

Hunger, Bladder, Energy, and Comfort are the most demanding of Motives, because if any one score drops below a certain level, the Sim will immediately exit his or her current activity to remedy the deficit. The following table lists the exit triggers for each category.

Mandatory Exit Factors

MOTIVE	SIM TYPE	EXITS CURRENT INTERACTION WHEN MOTIVE DROPS BELOW
Bladder	Resident	-85
Bladder	Visitor	-80
Comfort	Resident	-90
Comfort	Visitor	-60
Energy	Resident	-80
Energy	Visitor	-70
Hunger	Resident	-80
Hunger	Visitor	-40

Hygiene

Bad Hygiene will never kill a Sim, although it may seriously gross out others in the immediate vicinity. Solving this problem is easy—have your Sims wash their hands or take a shower. You can also combine Hygiene with other Motives. Taking a bath boosts the Hygiene and Comfort scores, while a soak in the hot tub (with friends) rewards the Hygiene, Comfort, Social, and Fun Motive bars.

Bladder

If you can't satisfy the Bladder urge, you'll be cleaning up puddles on the floor. Just make sure you find a bathroom before the Motive bar turns full red. A Sloppy Sim creates an additional risk by not regularly flushing the toilet. If you don't issue timely reminders, the toilet could get clogged, causing a major mess.

TIP

Pay special attention to the Bladder bar when your Sim spends time at the Beverage Bar or drinks a lot of coffee.

CAUTION

The Hygiene score takes a nose dive if a Sim can't get to the bathroom in time and pees on the floor.

Fig. 2-5. This Sim's Bladder is not quite full, but unless his guest vacates the bathroom soon, he could be in trouble.

Energy

We're talking sleep, pure and simple. Ideally, a good night's sleep should turn the bar completely green. This will happen at varying rates, depending upon the quality of the mattress, so you can get by on less sleep if you splurge for an expensive bed. If your Sim can't get to the bedroom or a couch before the Energy bar turns completely red, the floor becomes your only option. If this happens, wake your Sim and find the closest bed. A night on the hard floor will degrade your Sim's Comfort level to zero, while only restoring partial energy.

If your Sim stays up too late playing computer games, a shot of espresso provides a temporary Energy boost, although it will also fill the Bladder at an increased rate. Espresso has a powerful effect, but it takes longer to consume, which could be a problem if the car pool driver is honking.

Fig. 2-6. It never hurts to send your kids to bed early, because if they are tired in the morning, a coffee jolt is not an option.

Fun

Sims like to cut loose from the daily grind and have Fun, but depending upon their personalities, they prefer different activities. For example, a Playful Sim leans toward computer games, pinball machines, and train sets; while a more Serious Sim would rather sit down to a quiet game of chess or spend a few minutes gazing at a painting.

Fig. 2-7. These two Sims enjoy a game of pool after work.

Kids need to have more Fun than adults, and the effects of a single play session deteriorate faster for kids than for their older counterparts. Hence, it is a good idea to fill the house with plenty of juvenile diversions if you have children.

There are four different types of Fun activities: Extended, One-Time, Timed, and Endless. The following lists and tables provide additional information, including exit factors, for these pursuits.

Extended Fun Activities

Sims exit the following extended activities after reaching the maximum Fun score for their personality types. Hence, a Playful, Active Sim will stay on the basketball court longer than a Serious Sim.

- Basketball Hoop
- Bookshelf (reading)
- Dollhouse
- Computer (playing games)
- Pinball Machine
- Play Structure
- Stereo
- Toy Box
- Train Set
- TV
- VR Glasses

One-Time Fun Activities

The following activities raise a Sim's Fun score once with each interaction. It may take several interactions with the same activity for a Sim to reach the maximum Fun level.

OBJECT	ACTION
Aquarium	Feed or watch fish
Baby	Play
Diving Board	Dive into the pool
Espresso Machine	Drink espresso
Fountain	View
Lava Lamp	View
Painting	View
Sculpture	View

Timed (Pre-set) Fun Activities

As with the one-time activities listed above, a Sim may need to repeat the following activities to achieve maximum Fun points.

- Chess Set
- Pool Table

Endless Fun

- **Hot Tub:** A Sim will stay in the tub until Fun, Comfort, Social, and Hygiene numbers reach maximum levels.
- **Swimming Pool:** A Sim will keep doing laps until another Motive takes effect, or until you assign him or her to another activity.

Social

Sims crave other Sims, especially if they are Outgoing. Although they won't die without socializing, it is a good idea to devote a portion of each day to a group activity, even if it is a simple hot tub session with your Sim's mate, or a family meal.

Fig. 2-8. A casual conversation during breakfast raises this Sim's Social score.

The following table summarizes all of the possible Social interactions between adults and children. We take this one step further in the next chapter, "Interacting with Other Sims," where we examine Relationships.

Adult-Child Interactions

ACTION	ADULT TO ADULT	CHILD TO CHILD	ADULT TO CHILD	CHILD TO ADULT
Apologize	X	—	—	—
Attack	X	X	—	—
Brag	X	X	X	X
Call Here	X	X	X	X
Cheer Up	X	X	X	X
Compliment	X	—	—	—
Dance	X	—	—	—
Entertain	X	X	X	X
Flirt	X	—	—	—
Give Back Rub	X	—	—	—
Give Gift	X	X	X	X
Hug	X	X	X	X
Insult	X	X	X	X
Joke	X	X	X	X
Kiss	X	—	—	—
Say Goodbye	X	X	X	—
Scare	X	X	X	X
Slap	X	—	—	—
Tag	—	X	—	—
Talk	X	X	X	X
Tease	X	X	X	X
Tickle	X	X	X	X

Social Outcome Modifiers

You didn't expect a Sim Social encounter to be simple, did you? When one Sim communicates with another, several calculations determine the outcome. Factors include age (adult or child), sex, mood, and personality traits, not to mention the current state of their Relationship. Also, a Sim with strong Social needs (but few friends) may expect more from an encounter with a Sim who has similar needs.

The following table lists the factors that govern the choices that appear on a Social actions menu. For example, two Sims who are strangers are not likely to have the options to kiss or hug. Additionally, the table lists key factors that determine the eventual outcome.

rel =	Relationship
out =	Outgoing
play =	Playful
ff =	Friend Flag
ss =	Same Sex
rom =	Romance Flag
age =	Adult/Child
social =	Social Motive Value
vis =	Visitor
budget =	Household Budget
nice =	Nice
body =	Body

Social Outcome Factors

INTERACTION	FACTORS THAT DETERMINE APPEARANCE ON THE MENU	FACTORS THAT DETERMINE OUTCOME
Apologize	rel	mood
Attack	age, nice, mood, rel	body
Back Rub	age, nice, mood, rel, out, ss	rel, out, ss
Brag	nice, out, social, rel	rel, mood
Cheer Up	ff, mood (of friend), nice	rel
Compliment	age, nice, out, mood, rel	rel, mood
Dance	age, mood, out, rel	rel, out, mood
Entertain	social, out, play, mood, rel	play, rel
Flirt	age, social, ss, out, mood, rel, rom	rel, mood, ss
Gift	vis, budget, nice, mood, rel	rel, mood
Hug	age, out, mood, rel, ss	rel, out, mood, ss
Insult	nice, mood, rel	nice
Joke	play, mood, rel	play, mood, rel
Kiss	ss, mood, rel, age	rel, mood, ss
Scare	nice, mood, play, rel	play, mood
Slap	age, nice, mood, rel	nice, mood
Talk	mood, rel, out	topics match
Tease	nice, mood, rel	rel, mood
Tickle	social, out, play, active, mood, rel	rel, play

Room

This is a combined rating that analyzes the design and contents of the current room, and translates it into a Room score. Of all the Motives, Room is the least important. However, if you love your Sim, you'll want to create the best possible environment. The most important contributing factors to Room score are:

- **Light: Sims hate dark rooms, so fill your house with sunlight (windows and paned doors), lamps, and wall lights.**
- **Room Size: Don't cramp your Sims into tiny rooms.**
- **Corners: As mentioned in the "Building a House" chapter, Sims love corners.**
- **State of Repair: Any items that are not functioning properly detract from the Room score (see following list).**

Fig. 2-9. Who wouldn't love a kitchen like this? It's bright, roomy, nicely furnished, and packed with high-tech appliances.

Negative Impact on Room Score

- **Trash**
- **Floods**
- **Dirty plates**
- **Meals with flies**
- **Full trash cans/compactors**
- **Dead plants**
- **Puddle or ash pile**
- **Dead fish in aquariums**
- **Dirty objects (shower, toilet, tub)**

The following table lists the positive or negative value of every object in *The Sims*.

Room Score

OBJECT	STATE/TYPE	ROOM SCORE
Aquarium	Fish Alive	25
	Dirty	-25
	Dirty and/or Dead	-50
Ash	N/A	-10
Bar	N/A	20
Bed	Unmade (Any Bed)	-10
	Made Mission	30
	Made (Other than Mission)	10
Chair	Parisienne	25
	Empress	10
Clock (Grandfather)	N/A	50
Computer	Broken	-25
Counter	Barcelona	15
Desk	Redmond	15
Dresser	Antique Armoire	20
	Oak Armoire	10
Fire	N/A	-100

OBJECT	STATE/TYPE	ROOM SCORE
Fireplace	Library Edition (No Fire)	20
	Library Edition (Fire)	75
	Worcestershire (No Fire)	15
	Worcestershire (Fire)	60
	Bostonian (No Fire)	10
	Bostonian (Fire)	45
	Modesto (No Fire)	5
	Modesto (Fire)	30
Flamingo	N/A	10
Flood	N/A	-25
Flowers (Outdoor)	Healthy	20
	Dead	-20
Flowers/Plants (Indoor)	Healthy	10
	Wilted	0
	Dead	-10
Food	Snack (Spoiled)	-15
	Fruitcake (Empty Plate)	-5
	BBQ Group Meal (Spoiled)	-20
	BBQ Single Meal (Spoiled)	-15
	Empty Plate	-10
	Pizza Slice (Spoiled)	-10
	Pizza Box (Spoiled)	-25
	Candy (Spoiled)	-5
	Group Meal (Spoiled)	-20
	Meal (Spoiled)	-25
	Quick Meal (Spoiled)	-20
Fountain	N/A	25
Flowers (Gift)	Dead	-10
	Alive	20
Lamp	Not Broken	10
Lava Lamp	N/A	20
Newspaper	Old Newspapers	-20
Piano	N/A	30

OBJECT	STATE/TYPE	ROOM SCORE
Pinball Machine	Broken	-15
Shower	Broken	-15
Sofa (Deiter or Dolce)	N/A	20
Stereo	Strings	25
Table	Mesa	15
	Parisienne	25
Toilet	Clogged	-10
Train Set	Small	25
Trash Can (Inside)	Full	-20
Trash Compactor	Full	-25
Trash Pile	N/A	-20
TV	Soma	20
	Broken (Any TV)	-15

Object Advertising Values

Earlier in the chapter we mentioned that Sims receive Motive rewards when they select an activity. If you are in complete control of your Sims (Free Will is off), you determine their choices. However, with Free Will on, Sims constantly poll their surroundings to compare which objects are "advertising" the most attractive rewards. The following table includes a Motive profile of every object in *The Sims*.

Object Advertising Values

OBJECT TYPE	POSSIBLE INTERACTIONS	OBJECT VARIATIONS	ADVERTISED MOTIVE	ADVERTISED VALUE	PERSONALITY TRAIT MODIFIER	REDUCED EFFECTS (OVER DISTANCE)
Aquarium	Clean & Restock	N/A	Room	30	Neat	Medium
	Feed Fish	N/A	Room	10	Nice	High
		N/A	Fun	10	Playful	High
	Watch Fish	N/A	Fun	10	Playful	High
Ash	Sweep Up	N/A	Energy	23	N/A	Medium
		N/A	Room	50	Neat	Medium
Baby	Play	N/A	Fun	50	Playful	Medium
Bar	Have Drink	N/A	Room	30	N/A	Low
	Grill	Barbecue	Energy	-10	N/A	Low
			Hunger	40	Cooking	Low
Basketball Hoop	Join	N/A	Fun	30	Active	High
		N/A	Social	20	N/A	Medium
		N/A	Energy	-20	N/A	Medium
	Play	N/A	Fun	30	Active	High
		N/A	Energy	-20	N/A	High
Bed	Make Bed	All Beds	Room	25	Neat	High
	Sleep	Double Bed (Cheap Eazzzzze)	Energy	65	N/A	None
		Double Bed (Napoleon)	Energy	67	N/A	None
		Double Bed (Mission)	Energy	70	N/A	None
		Single Bed (Spartan)	Energy	60	N/A	None
		Single Bed (Tyke Nyte)	Energy	63	N/A	None
	Tuck in Kid	All Beds	Energy	160	Nice	None

OBJECT TYPE	POSSIBLE INTERACTIONS	OBJECT VARIATIONS	ADVERTISED MOTIVE	ADVERTISED VALUE	PERSONALITY TRAIT MODIFIER	REDUCED EFFECTS (OVER DISTANCE)
Bookcase	Read a Book	Bookcase (Pine)	Fun	10	Serious	High
		Bookcase (Amishim)	Fun	20	Serious	High
		Bookcase (Libri di Regina)	Fun	30	Serious	High
Chair (Living Room)	Sit	Wicker	Comfort	20	N/A	Medium
		Country Class	Comfort	20	N/A	Medium
		Citronel	Comfort	20	N/A	Medium
		Sarrbach	Comfort	20	N/A	Medium
Chair (Dining Room)	Sit	Werkbunnst	Comfort	25	N/A	Medium
		Teak	Comfort	25	N/A	Medium
		Empress	Comfort	25	N/A	Medium
		Parisienne	Comfort	25	N/A	Medium
Chair (Office/Deck)	Sit	Office Chair	Comfort	20	N/A	Medium
		Deck Chair	Comfort	20	N/A	Medium
Chair (Recliner)	Nap	Both Recliners	Energy	15	Lazy	High
		Both Recliners	Comfort	20	Lazy	Medium
	Sit	Both Recliners	Comfort	30	Lazy	Medium
Chess	Join	Chess Set	Fun	40	Outgoing	High
			Social	40	N/A	Medium
	Play		Fun	35	Serious	High
Clock (Grandfather)	Wind	N/A	Room	40	Neat	High
Coffee (Espresso Machine)	Drink Espresso	N/A	Energy	115	N/A	Medium
		N/A	Fun	10	N/A	High
		N/A	Bladder	-10	N/A	High
Coffeemaker	Drink Coffee	N/A	Bladder	-5	N/A	High
		N/A	Energy	115	N/A	Medium

OBJECT TYPE	POSSIBLE INTERACTIONS	OBJECT VARIATIONS	ADVERTISED MOTIVE	ADVERTISED VALUE	PERSONALITY TRAIT MODIFIER	REDUCED EFFECTS (OVER DISTANCE)
Computer	Play	Moneywell	Fun	30	Playful	High
		Microscotch	Fun	35	Playful	High
		Brahma	Fun	40	Playful	High
		Marco	Fun	50	Playful	High
	Turn Off	All Computers	Energy	220	Neat	Medium
Dollhouse	Play	N/A	Fun	30	Playful	High
	Watch	N/A	Fun	30	Playful	Medium
		N/A	Social	30	N/A	Medium
Easel	Paint	N/A	Fun	20	N/A	High
Flamingo	Kick	N/A	Mood	15	Grouchy	High
	View	N/A	Fun	10	Playful	High
Flood	Clean	N/A	Room	80	Neat	High
Flowers (Outdoor)	Stomp On	N/A	Mood	10	Grouchy	High
	Water	N/A	Room	20	Neat	Medium
Flowers/Plants (Indoor)	Throw Out	N/A	Room	50	Neat	Medium
	Water	N/A	Room	25	Neat	Medium
Food	Clean	All Meal/ Snack Types	Room	20	Neat	Medium
	Prepare and Eat	BBQ Group Meal	Hunger	90	N/A	Low
		BBQ Single	Hunger	80	N/A	Low
		Candy	Hunger	30	N/A	Low
		Fruitcake (Group Meal)	Hunger	30	N/A	Low
		Fruitcake (Slice)	Hunger	80	N/A	Low
		Light Meal	Hunger	80	N/A	Low
		Pizza Box	Hunger	90	N/A	Low
		Pizza Slice	Hunger	80	N/A	Low
		Regular Group Meal	Hunger	90	N/A	Low
		Regular Single Meal	Hunger	80	N/A	Low
		Snack	Hunger	25	N/A	Low

OBJECT TYPE	POSSIBLE INTERACTIONS	OBJECT VARIATIONS	ADVERTISED MOTIVE	ADVERTISED VALUE	PERSONALITY TRAIT MODIFIER	REDUCED EFFECTS (OVER DISTANCE)
Fountain	Play	N/A	Fun	10	Shy	High
Refrigerator	Have Meal	All Fridges	Hunger	65	N/A	Low
	Have Snack	Llamark	Hunger	20	N/A	Low
		Porcina	Hunger	30	N/A	Low
		Freeze Secret	Hunger	40	N/A	Low
	Have Quick Meal	All Fridges	Hunger	55	N/A	Low
	Serve Meal	All Fridges	Hunger	70	Cooking	Low
		All Fridges	Energy	-10	N/A	Low
Gift (Flowers)	Clean	N/A	Room	30	Neat	Medium
Hot Tub	Get In	N/A	Fun	45	Lazy	High
		N/A	Comfort	50	N/A	High
		N/A	Social	25	Outgoing	Medium
		N/A	Hygiene	5	N/A	Medium
	Join	N/A	Comfort	30	N/A	Low
		N/A	Fun	50	Outgoing	Low
		N/A	Social	50	N/A	Low
		N/A	Hygiene	5	N/A	Medium
Lava Lamp	Turn On	N/A	Room	5	N/A	High
		N/A	Fun	5	N/A	High
Mailbox	Get Mail	N/A	Comfort	10	N/A	High
		N/A	Hunger	10	N/A	High
		N/A	Hygiene	10	N/A	High
		N/A	Room	10	N/A	High
Medicine Cabinet	Brush Teeth	N/A	Hygiene	25	Neat	Medium
Newspaper	Clean Up	N/A	Room	50	Neat	Medium
	Read	N/A	Fun	5	Serious	High
Painting	View	N/A	Fun	5	Serious	High
Phone	Answer	N/A	Fun	50	N/A	Medium
		N/A	Comfort	50	N/A	Medium
		N/A	Social	50	N/A	Medium
Piano	Play	N/A	Fun	40	Strong Creativity	High
	Watch	N/A	Fun	70	N/A	Medium
		N/A	Social	10	N/A	Medium

OBJECT TYPE	POSSIBLE INTERACTIONS	OBJECT VARIATIONS	ADVERTISED MOTIVE	ADVERTISED VALUE	PERSONALITY TRAIT MODIFIER	REDUCED EFFECTS (OVER DISTANCE)
Pinball Machine	Join	N/A	Fun	50	N/A	Medium
		N/A	Social	30	N/A	Medium
	Play	N/A	Fun	40	Playful	High
Play Structure	Join	N/A	Fun	60	Playful	Medium
		N/A	Social	40	N/A	Medium
	Play	N/A	Fun	60	Playful	Medium
Pool Diving Board	Dive In	N/A	Fun	35	Active	High
		N/A	Energy	-10	N/A	High
Pool Table	Join	N/A	Fun	50	Playful	Low
		N/A	Social	40	N/A	Low
	Play	N/A	Fun	45	Playful	High
Sculpture	View	Scylla and Charybdis	Fun	6	Serious	High
		Bust of Athena	Fun	5	Serious	High
		Large Black Slab	Fun	8	Serious	High
		China Vase	Fun	7	Serious	High
Shower	Clean	N/A	Room	20	Neat	High
	Take a Shower	N/A	Hygiene	50	Neat	Medium
Sink	Wash Hands	N/A	Hygiene	10	Neat	High
Sofa/Loveseat	Nap	All Sofas/ Loveseats	Energy	40	Lazy	High
		All Sofas/ Loveseats	Comfort	5	Lazy	High
	Sit	All Sofas/ Loveseats	Comfort	30	Lazy	Medium
		Garden Bench	Comfort	30	Lazy	Medium
Stereo	Dance	Boom Box	Social	40	Outgoing	High
			Fun	50	Active	High
		Zimantz Hi-Fi	Social	50	Outgoing	High
			Fun	60	Active	High
		Strings Theory	Social	60	Outgoing	High
			Fun	70	Active	High
	Join	Boom Box	Social	40	Outgoing	Low

OBJECT TYPE	POSSIBLE INTERACTIONS	OBJECT VARIATIONS	ADVERTISED MOTIVE	ADVERTISED VALUE	PERSONALITY TRAIT MODIFIER	REDUCED EFFECTS (OVER DISTANCE)
Stereo			Fun	40	Outgoing	Low
		Zimantz Hi-Fi	Social	50	Outgoing	Low
			Fun	40	Outgoing	Low
		Strings Theory	Social	60	Outgoing	Low
			Fun	40	Outgoing	Low
	Turn Off	All Stereos	Energy	220	Neat	Medium
	Turn On	Boom Box	Fun	25	Playful	High
		Zimantz Hi-Fi	Fun	25	Playful	High
		Strings Theory	Fun	30	Playful	High
Toilet	Clean	Both Toilets	Room	40	Neat	High
	Flush	Hygeia-O-Matic	Room	30	Neat	High
	Unclog	Both Toilets	Room	50	Neat	High
	Use	Hygeia-O-Matic	Bladder	50	N/A	Low
		Flush Force	Bladder	70	N/A	Low
Tombstone/ Urn	Mourn (first 24 hours)	N/A	Bladder	5	N/A	Low
		N/A	Comfort	50	N/A	Low
		N/A	Energy	5	N/A	Low
		N/A	Fun	50	N/A	Low
		N/A	Hunger	5	N/A	Low
		N/A	Hygiene	50	N/A	Low
		N/A	Social	50	N/A	Low
		N/A	Room	50	N/A	Low
	Mourn (second 48 hours)	N/A	Bladder	0	N/A	Low
		N/A	Comfort	30	N/A	Low
		N/A	Energy	0	N/A	Low
		N/A	Fun	30	N/A	Low
		N/A	Hunger	0	N/A	Low
		N/A	Hygiene	30	N/A	Low
		N/A	Social	30	N/A	Low
		N/A	Room	30	N/A	Low
Toy Box	Play	N/A	Fun	55	Playful	Medium

OBJECT TYPE	POSSIBLE INTERACTIONS	OBJECT VARIATIONS	ADVERTISED MOTIVE	ADVERTISED VALUE	PERSONALITY TRAIT MODIFIER	REDUCED EFFECTS (OVER DISTANCE)
Train Set (Large)	Play	N/A	Fun	40	N/A	Medium
	Watch	N/A	Fun	40	N/A	Low
		N/A	Social	40	N/A	Low
Train Set (Small)	Play	N/A	Fun	45	Playful	Medium
	Watch	N/A	Fun	20	N/A	Medium
		N/A	Social	30	N/A	Medium
Trash Can (Inside)	Empty Trash	N/A	Room	30	Neat	Medium
Trash Compactor	Empty Trash	N/A	Room	30	N/A	High
Trash Pile	Clean	N/A	Room	75	Neat	Medium
Bathtub	Clean	All Tubs	Room	20	Neat	High
	Bathe	Justa	Hygiene	50	Neat	Medium
		Justa	Comfort	20	N/A	Medium
		Sani-Queen	Hygiene	60	Neat	Medium
		Sani-Queen	Comfort	25	N/A	Medium
		Hydrothera	Hygiene	70	Neat	Medium
		Hydrothera	Comfort	30	N/A	Medium
TV	Join	Monochrome	Fun	20	Lazy	High
		Trottco	Fun	30	Lazy	High
		Soma Plasma	Fun	45	Lazy	High
	Turn Off	All TVs	Energy	220	Neat	Medium
	Turn On	Monochrome	Fun	18	Lazy	High
		Trottco	Fun	35	Lazy	High
		Soma Plasma	Fun	49	Lazy	High
	Watch TV	Monochrome	Fun	18	Lazy	High
		Trottco	Fun	28	Lazy	High
		Soma Plasma	Fun	42	Lazy	High
VR Glasses	Play	N/A	Fun	60	Playful	High

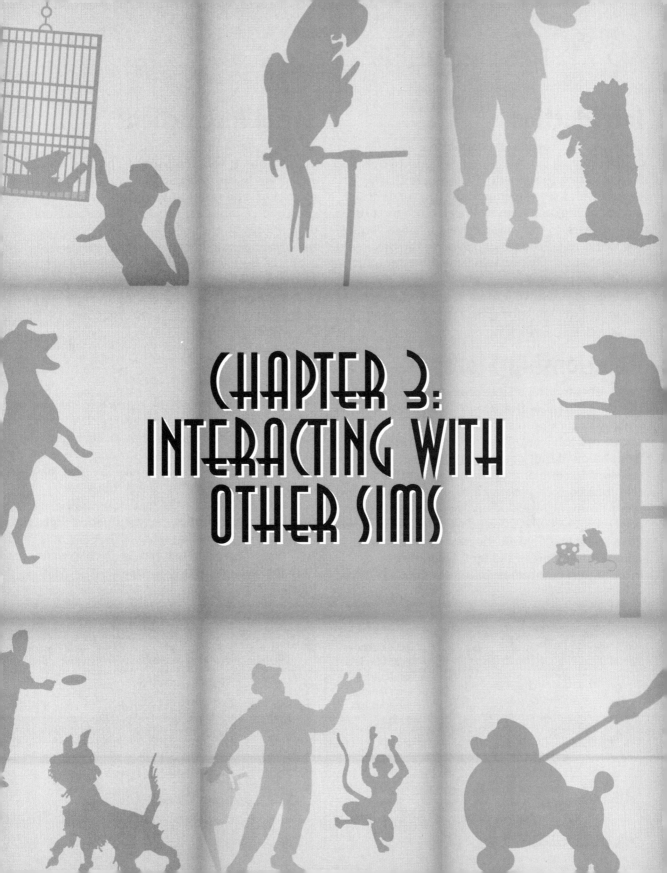

CHAPTER 3: INTERACTING WITH OTHER SIMS

Introduction

Once you get beyond the dark attraction of watching jilted Sims slap their rivals, or obnoxious Sims insulting their friends, you realize that Relationships are very important to your Sims' quality of life, and even to the advancement of their careers. In this chapter, we introduce you to the world of Relationships, covering the possible events that occur when two Sims come together verbally or physically. Our goal here is to lay down the ground rules. We'll offer hands-on tips for building and maintaining Relationships in the "All in the Family" chapter.

Relationship Scores

Icons representing a Sim's friendships, or lack thereof, appear in the screen's lower-right corner when you click on the Relationships icon (just above the Job icon). The scoring system ranges from below 0 (not good) to 100, which is reserved for one or more significant others. A relationship is considered a true friendship if the score climbs above 50. Only these Relationships are considered when the game calculates career advancements. Consult the next chapter, "9 to 5: Climbing the Career Ladder," for more information on promotion requirements.

Social Interactions

All Sim Relationships develop from Social interactions. If you don't spend quality time with your friends, the Relationships will deteriorate on their own, at a rate of two points per day. Of course, if you interact poorly, the rate accelerates dramatically. In the following sections, we review the myriad communication choices that are available during the game (grouped alphabetically by the active action). At any given time, your choice will vary, depending upon the level of your friendship, and whether or not your Sim is acting like a jerk!

Good Old Conversation

The easiest way to cultivate a new friendship is to talk. Sims communicate with each either using Sim-Speak, a delightful chatter that you actually begin to understand (yes, we have played this game way too much!). Adults and kids have favorite topics within their peer groups. These topics are randomly assigned by the game during the Sim creation process. Additionally, kids and adults have special cross-generational topics that are only used with each other. Active topics are displayed in thought balloons during the game, as shown in figure 3-2.

Fig. 3-1. This Sim Dad is clicking on all cylinders with his wife, but he needs to spend more time with the kids.

Fig. 3-2. Pets are a good common ground for conversation between adults and kids.

When a conversation is going well, you see a green plus sign over one or both of the Sims. Conversely, when talk deteriorates into the gutter, you'll see red minus signs. The following tables list positive and negative communications, including each potential outcome and the corresponding effect on Social and Relationship scores. For our purposes, an outcome is positive if it produces an increase in one or both scores. When scores drop or stay the same, it is considered a negative outcome.

Fig. 3-3. When two or more people enter a hot tub, the conversations begin spontaneously.

Positive Communications

INTERACTION	RESPONSE	RELATIONSHIP CHANGE	SOCIAL SCORE CHANGE
Apologize	Accept	10	15
Be Apologized To	Accept	10	15
Brag	Good	5	13
Be Bragged To	Good	5	7
Cheer Up	Good	5	7
Cheer Up	Neutral	0	5
Be Cheered Up	Good	10	10
Be Cheered Up	Neutral	0	5
Compliment	Accept	5	5
Be Complimented	Accept	5	11
Entertain	Laugh	4	7
Be Entertained	Laugh	8	13
Flirt	Good	5	13
Be Flirted With	Good	10	13
Joke	Laugh	5	13
Joke	Giggle	2	7
Listen to Joke	Laugh	7	13
Listen to Joke	Giggle	3	7
Scare	Laugh	5	10
TalkHigh Interest	Topic	3	5
TalkLike	Topic	3	5
Group Talk	N/A	1	8
Tease	Giggle	5	7

Negative Communications

INTERACTION	RESPONSE	RELATIONSHIP CHANGE	SOCIAL SCORE CHANGE
Apologize	Reject	-10	0
Be Apologized To	Reject	-10	0
Brag	Bad	-5	0
Be Bragged To	Bad	-5	0
Cheer Up	Bad	-3	0
Be Cheered Up	Bad	-10	0
Compliment	Reject	-10	0
Be Complimented	Reject	-7	0
Entertain	Boo	-15	0
Be Entertained	Boo	-7	0
Flirt	Refuse	-10	-17
Flirt	Ignore	-5	0
Be Flirted With	Refuse	-10	0
Be Flirted With	Ignore	0	0
Insult	Cry	5	0
Insult	Stoic	0	3
Insult	Angry	-10	7
Be Insulted	Cry	-12	-13
Be Insulted	Stoic	-5	-5
Be Insulted	Angry	-14	-7
Joke	Uninterested	-6	0
Listen to Joke	Uninterested	-7	0
Scare	Angry	-5	0
Be Scared	Angry	-10	0
TalkDislike	Topic	-3	3
TalkHate	Topic	-3	3
Tease	Cry	-4	0
Be Teased	Cry	-13	-7

Physical Contact

When a Relationship moves past the 50-point threshold, you begin to see new options on the Social interaction menu. Instead of just talking, you find new items including Hug, Give Back Rub, Flirt, and Kiss. It all depends upon how your Relationship is progressing and what the other Sim is looking for in the current interaction. The following tables include information on positive and negative physical events.

Positive Physical Events

INTERACTION	RESPONSE	RELATIONSHIP CHANGE	SOCIAL SCORE CHANGE
Give Back Rub	Good	5	7
Receive Back Rub	Good	9	13
Dance	Accept	8	13
Be Danced With	Accept	10	13
Give Gift	Accept	5	7
Receive Gift	Accept	10	13
Hug	Good	7	15
Hug	Tentative	2	7
Be Hugged	Good	8	15
Be Hugged	Tentative	4	7
Kiss	Passion	12	20
Kiss	Polite	5	10
Be Kissed	Passion	12	20
Be Kissed	Polite	5	10
Tickle	Accept	5	13
Be Tickled	Accept	8	13

Negative Physical Events

INTERACTION	RESPONSE	RELATIONSHIP CHANGE	SOCIAL SCORE CHANGE
Attack	Win Fight	-5	10
Attack	Lose Fight	-10	-20
Give Back Rub	Bad	-7	0
Receive Back Rub	Bad	-10	0
Dance	Refuse	-5	0
Be Danced With	Refuse	-5	0
Give Gift	Stomp	-15	0
Receive Gift	Stomp	-5	0
Hug	Refuse	-10	0
Be Hugged	Refuse	-10	0
Kiss	Deny	-15	5
Be Kissed	Deny	-10	0
Slap	Cry	0	3
Slap	Slap Back	-10	-7
Be Slapped	Cry	-20	-17
Be Slapped	Slap Back	-15	7
Tickle	Refuse	-5	0
Be Tickled	Refuse	-8	0

CHAPTER 4:
9 TO 5—CLIMBING THE CAREER LADDER

Introduction

When you first start playing *The Sims*, it's easy to get lost in the element. There's so much to explore and experience, and with more than enough money to furnish your house and buy a few toys, you can just hang out and live the good Sim-life. But, reality sets in sooner than you would like, and you must find a job. In this chapter we show you how to select a career, nurture the Skills necessary to earn the first few promotions, and finally, stockpile enough friends (it's called networking) to make the big bucks and zoom to the top of your field. For easy reference, we include comprehensive career tables that contain everything you need to know about the 10 Sim careers, including advancement requirements for all 10 pay levels.

Your First Job

Every Sim house receives a daily copy of the *Sim City Times* that includes a single job posting. You can take the first job you see, or buy a computer and view three jobs a day. There is no rush—you have enough money to get by for several days.

TIP

You can enjoy the free use of a computer by buying it, checking the want ads, and then returning it the same day for a full refund. Keep this up until you find the job you want. Then, later when you have more disposable cash, you can buy—and keep—a computer.

A Military job is usually available on the computer. This is an excellent first career, with a starting salary of §250. Furthermore, it remains the highest paying of the 10 careers through the first three advances. A Law Enforcement position is a close second.

Fig. 4-2. This two-commando family takes home §325 each as members of the Elite Forces (Level 2—Military Career).

If you would rather take your time and sort through all 10 job tracks, the following table will help you choose a career that is suited to your Sim's personality traits.

Fig. 4-1. Today's job posting is for a test driver.

Career Choices

CAREER TRACK	NECESSARY SKILLS	RELATED PERSONALITY TRAITS
Business	Logic, Charisma	Outgoing
Entertainment	Charisma, Creativity	Outgoing, Playful
Law Enforcement	Logic, Body	Active
Life of Crime	Creativity, Charisma	Playful, Outgoing
Medicine	Logic, Body	Active
Military	Repair, Body	Active
Politics	Charisma, Logic	Outgoing
Pro Athlete	Body, Charisma	Active, Outgoing
Science	Logic, Creativity	Playful
Xtreme	Creativity, Body/Charisma (tie)	Playful, Active, Outgoing

Developing Your Skills

After you decide on a career, focus on developing the appropriate Skills needed for advancement. It is important to remember that Sims do not study on their own. You need to direct your Sim to one of the activities listed in the Skill Enhancement table below.

TIP

On the control panel, click on the Job icon to display your Sim's current Skill bars (see figure 4-3). A white line designates the minimum level of Skill needed for the next promotion. Other factors contribute to earning a promotion, but without the Skill requirement, you have absolutely no chance for advancement to the next level.

Fig. 4-3. This Sim needs to boost his Body Skill one more notch, so he is scheduled for a session on the exercise machine right after lunch.

Skill Enhancement

SKILL	METHOD OF ENHANCEMENT	NOTES
Cooking	Bookshelf (Study Cooking)	Any type of bookshelf will suffice.
Mechanical	Bookshelf (Study Mechanical)	Any type of bookshelf will suffice.
Body	Exercise Machine (Work Out)	Exercise machine increases Skill four times faster than the pool. Active Sims improve their Skill at a higher rate.
	Pool (Swim)	See above.
Charisma	Mirrors or Medicine Cabinet (Practice Speech)	Outgoing Sims acquire Skill more quickly.
	Easel (Paint)	Playful Sims acquire Skill more quickly.
	Piano (Play)	Playful Sims acquire Skill more quickly.
Logic	Chessboard (Play)	Playing with another Sim generates Social points.

Fig. 4-4. A session on the exercise bench nets a Body point for this Sim.

Sim Career Tracks

The following tables include the salaries, hours, car pool vehicles, and job level requirements for each level of the 10 Sim career tracks. The Daily Motive Decay value shows which Motives deteriorate while the Sim is on the job.

Requirements for Level 1 Positions

CAREER TRACK	POSITION	PAY	HOURS	CAR POOL VEHICLE	COOKING	REPAIR	CHARISMA	BODY	LOGIC	CREATIVITY	FAMILY/ FRIENDS	DAILY MOTIVE DECAY						
												HUNGER	COMFORT	HYGIENE	BLADDER	ENERGY	FUN	SOCIAL
Business	Mail Room	§120	9 a.m.–3 p.m.	Junker	0	0	0	0	0	0	0	0	0	0	0	-30	0	0
Entertainment	Waiter Waitress	§100	9 a.m.–3 p.m.	Junker	0	0	0	0	0	0	0	0	0	0	0	-30	0	0
Law Enforcement	Security Guard	§240	12 a.m.–6 a.m.	Squad Car	0	0	0	0	0	0	0	0	0	0	0	-30	0	0
Life of Crime	Pickpocket	§140	9 a.m.–3 p.m.	Junker	0	0	0	0	0	0	0	0	0	0	0	-30	0	0
Medicine	Medical Technician	§200	9 a.m.–3 p.m.	Junker	0	0	0	0	0	0	0	0	0	0	0	-30	0	0
Military	Recruit	§250	6 a.m.–12 p.m.	Military Jeep	0	0	0	0	0	0	0	0	0	-15	0	-30	0	0
Politics	Campaign Work	§220	9 a.m.–6 p.m.	Junker	0	0	0	0	0	0	0	0	0	0	0	-30	0	0
Pro Athlete	Team Mascot	§110	12 p.m.–6 p.m.	Junker	0	0	0	0	0	0	0	0	0	-5	0	-35	0	0
Science	Test Subject	§155	9 a.m.–3 p.m.	Junker	0	0	0	0	0	0	0	0	0	0	0	-30	0	0
Xtreme	Daredevil	§175	9 a.m.–3 p.m.	Junker	0	0	0	0	0	0	0	0	0	0	0	-30	0	0

Requirements for Level 2 Positions

CAREER TRACK	POSITION	PAY	HOURS	CAR POOL VEHICLE	COOKING	REPAIR	CHARISMA	BODY	LOGIC	CREATIVITY	FAMILY/ FRIENDS	DAILY MOTIVE DECAY						
												HUNGER	COMFORT	HYGIENE	BLADDER	ENERGY	FUN	SOCIAL
Business	Executive Assistant	§180	9 a.m.–4 p.m.	Junker	0	0	0	0	0	0	0	0	0	0	0	-34	-2	0
Entertainment	Extra	§150	9 a.m.–3 p.m.	Junker	0	0	0	0	0	0	0	0	0	0	0	-34	-2	0
Law Enforcement	Cadet	§320	9 a.m.–3 p.m.	Squad Car	0	0	0	0	0	0	0	0	0	0	0	-34	-2	0
Life of Crime	Bagman	§200	11 p.m.–7 a.m.	Junker	0	0	0	0	0	0	0	0	0	0	0	-34	-2	0
Medicine	Paramedic	§275	11 p.m.–5 a.m.	Junker	0	0	0	0	0	0	0	0	0	0	0	-34	-2	0
Military	Elite Forces	§325	7 a.m.–1 p.m.	Military Jeep	0	0	0	0	0	0	0	0	0	-15	0	-34	-2	0
Politics	Intern	§300	9 a.m.–3 p.m.	Junker	0	0	0	0	0	0	0	0	0	0	0	-34	-2	0
Pro Athlete	Minor Leaguer	§170	9 a.m.–3 p.m.	Junker	0	0	0	0	0	0	0	0	0	-10	0	-40	-2	0
Science	Lab Assistant	§230	11 p.m.–5 a.m.	Junker	0	0	0	0	0	0	0	0	0	0	0	-34	-2	0
Xtreme	Bungee Jump Instructor	§250	9 a.m.–3 p.m.	Junker	0	0	0	0	0	0	0	0	0	0	0	-34	-2	0

Requirements for Level 3 Positions

CAREER TRACK	POSITION	PAY	HOURS	CAR POOL VEHICLE	COOKING	REPAIR	CHARISMA	BODY	LOGIC	CREATIVITY	FAMILY/ FRIENDS	DAILY MOTIVE DECAY						
												HUNGER	COMFORT	HYGIENE	BLADDER	ENERGY	FUN	SOCIAL
Business	Field Sales Rep	§250	9 a.m. –4 p.m.	Junker	0	2	0	0	0	0	0	-3	0	-5	0	-38	-4	0
Entertainment	Bit Player	§200	9 a.m. –3 p.m.	Junker	0	0	2	0	0	0	0	-3	0	-5	0	-38	-4	0
Law Enforcement	Patrol Officer	§380	5 p.m. –1 a.m.	Squad Car	0	0	0	2	0	0	0	-3	0	-5	0	-38	-4	0
Life of Crime	Bookie	§275	12 p.m. –7 p.m.	Standard Car	0	0	0	2	0	0	0	-3	0	-5	0	-38	-4	0
Medicine	Nurse	§340	9 a.m. –3 p.m.	Standard Car	0	2	0	0	0	0	0	-3	0	-5	0	-38	-4	0
Military	Drill Instructor	§250	8 a.m. –2 p.m.	Military Jeep	0	0	0	2	0	0	0	-3	0	-20	0	-38	-4	0
Politics	Lobbyist	§360	9 a.m. –3 p.m.	Standard Car	0	0	2	0	0	0	0	-3	0	-5	0	-38	-4	0
Pro Athlete	Rookie	§230	9 a.m. –3 p.m.	Junker	0	0	0	2	0	0	0	-3	0	-15	0	-45	-2	0
Science	Field Researcher	§320	9 a.m. –3 p.m.	Standard Car	0	0	0	0	2	0	0	-3	0	-5	0	-38	-4	0
Xtreme	Whitewater Guide	§325	9 a.m. –3 p.m.	SUV	0	0	0	2	0	0	1	-3	0	-10	0	-45	-4	0

Requirements for Level 4 Positions

CAREER TRACK	POSITION	PAY	HOURS	CAR POOL VEHICLE	COOKING	REPAIR	CHARISMA	BODY	LOGIC	CREATIVITY	FAMILY/ FRIENDS	DAILY MOTIVE DECAY						
												HUNGER	COMFORT	HYGIENE	BLADDER	ENERGY	FUN	SOCIAL
Business	Junior Executive	§320	9 a.m. –4 p.m.	Standard Car	0	2	2	0	0	0	1	-7	0	-10	0	-42	-7	0
Entertainment	Stunt Double	§275	9 a.m. –4 p.m.	Standard Car	0	0	2	2	0	0	2	-7	0	-10	0	-42	-7	0
Law Enforcement	Desk Sergeant	§440	9 a.m. –3 p.m.	Squad Car	0	2	0	2	0	0	1	-7	0	-10	0	-42	-7	0
Life of Crime	Con Artist	§350	9 a.m. –3 p.m.	Standard Car	0	0	1	2	0	1	2	-7	0	-10	0	-42	-7	0
Medicine	Intern	§410	9 a.m. –6 p.m.	Standard Car	0	2	0	2	0	0	2	-7	0	-10	0	-42	-7	0
Military	Junior Officer	§450	9 a.m. –3 p.m.	Military Jeep	0	1	2	2	0	0	0	-7	0	-20	0	-42	-8	0
Politics	Campaign Manager	§430	9 a.m. –6 p.m.	Standard Car	0	0	2	0	1	0	2	-7	0	-10	0	-42	-7	0
Pro Athlete	Starter	§300	9 a.m. –3 p.m.	Standard Car	0	0	0	5	0	0	1	-7	0	-20	0	-50	-2	0
Science	Science Teacher	§375	9 a.m. –4 p.m.	Standard Car	0	0	1	0	3	0	1	-7	0	-10	0	-40	-7	0
Xtreme	Xtreme Circuit Pro	§400	9 a.m. –3 p.m.	SUV	0	1	0	4	0	0	2	-7	0	-20	0	-50	-2	0

Requirements for Level 5 Positions

CAREER TRACK	POSITION	PAY	HOURS	CAR POOL VEHICLE	COOKING	REPAIR	CHARISMA	BODY	LOGIC	CREATIVITY	FAMILY/ FRIENDS	DAILY MOTIVE DECAY						
												HUNGER	COMFORT	HYGIENE	BLADDER	ENERGY	FUN	SOCIAL
Business	Executive	§400	9 a.m.–4 p.m.	Standard Car	0	2	2	0	2	0	3	-10	0	-15	0	-46	-10	0
Entertainment	B-Movie Star	§375	10 a.m.–5 p.m.	Standard Car	0	0	3	3	0	1	4	-10	0	-15	0	-46	-10	0
Law Enforcement	Vice Squad	§490	10 p.m.–4 a.m.	Squad Car	0	3	0	4	0	0	2	-10	0	-15	0	-46	-10	0
Life of Crime	Getaway Driver	§425	5 p.m.–1 a.m.	Standard Car	0	2	1	2	0	2	3	-10	0	-10	0	-46	-10	0
Medicine	Resident	§480	9 p.m.–4 a.m.	Standard Car	0	3	0	2	2	0	3	-10	0	-15	0	-46	-10	0
Military	Counter-Intelligence	§500	9 a.m.–3 p.m.	Military Jeep	1	1	2	4	0	0	0	-10	0	-25	0	-46	-12	0
Politics	City Council Member	§485	9 a.m.–3 p.m.	Town Car	0	0	3	1	1	0	4	-10	0	-15	0	-46	-8	0
Pro Athlete	All-Star	§385	9 a.m.–3 p.m.	SUV	0	1	1	6	0	0	3	-10	0	-25	0	-55	-3	0
Science	Project Leader	§450	9 a.m.–5 p.m.	Standard Car	0	0	2	0	4	1	3	-10	0	-12	0	-43	-8	0
Xtreme	Bush Pilot	§475	9 a.m.–3 p.m.	SUV	1	2	0	4	1	0	3	-10	0	-15	0	-46	-5	-10

Requirements for Level 6 Positions

CAREER TRACK	POSITION	PAY	HOURS	CAR POOL VEHICLE	COOKING	REPAIR	CHARISMA	BODY	LOGIC	CREATIVITY	FAMILY/ FRIENDS	DAILY MOTIVE DECAY						
												HUNGER	COMFORT	HYGIENE	BLADDER	ENERGY	FUN	SOCIAL
Business	Senior Manager	§520	9 a.m.–4 p.m.	Standard Car	0	2	3	0	3	2	6	-14	0	-20	0	-50	-13	0
Entertainment	Supporting Player	§500	10 a.m.–6 p.m.	Limo	0	1	4	4	0	2	6	-14	0	-20	0	-50	-13	0
Law Enforcement	Detective	§540	9 a.m.–3 p.m.	Squad Car	1	3	1	5	1	0	4	-14	0	-20	0	-50	-13	0
Life of Crime	Bank Robber	§530	3 p.m.–11 p.m.	Town Car	0	3	2	3	1	2	4	-14	0	-15	0	-50	-13	-5
Medicine	GP	§550	10 a.m.–6 p.m.	Town Car	0	3	1	3	4	0	4	-14	0	-20	0	-50	-13	0
Military	Flight Officer	§550	9 a.m.–3 p.m.	Military Jeep	1	2	4	4	1	0	1	-14	0	-28	0	-50	-15	0
Politics	State Assembly-person	§540	9 a.m.–4 p.m.	Town Car	0	0	4	2	1	1	6	-14	0	-20	0	-50	-12	-3
Pro Athlete	MVP	§510	9 a.m.–3 p.m.	SUV	0	2	2	7	0	0	5	-14	0	-30	0	-60	-4	0
Science	Inventor	§540	10 a.m.–7 p.m.	Town Car	0	2	2	0	4	3	4	-14	0	-15	0	-45	-9	-8
Xtreme	Mountain Climber	§550	9 a.m.–3 p.m.	SUV	1	4	0	6	1	0	4	-14	0	-30	0	-60	0	0

Requirements for Level 7 Positions

CAREER TRACK	POSITION	PAY	HOURS	CAR POOL VEHICLE	COOKING	REPAIR	CHARISMA	BODY	LOGIC	CREATIVITY	FAMILY/ FRIENDS	HUNGER	COMFORT	HYGIENE	BLADDER	ENERGY	FUN	SOCIAL
Business	Vice President	§660	9 a.m.–5 p.m.	Town Car	0	2	4	2	4	2	8	-18	0	-25	0	-54	-16	0
Entertainment	TV Star	§650	10 a.m.–6 p.m.	Limo	0	1	6	5	0	3	8	-18	0	-25	0	-54	-16	0
Law Enforcement	Lieutenant	§590	9 a.m.–3 p.m.	Limo	1	3	2	5	3	1	6	-18	0	-25	0	-54	-16	0
Life of Crime	Cat Burglar	§640	9 p.m.–3 a.m.	Town Car	1	3	2	5	2	3	6	-18	0	-20	0	-54	-16	0
Medicine	Specialist	§625	10 p.m.–4 a.m.	Town Car	0	4	2	4	4	1	5	-18	0	-25	0	-54	-16	0
Military	Senior Officer	§580	9 a.m.–3 p.m.	Military Jeep	1	3	4	5	3	0	3	-18	0	-31	0	-55	-20	0
Politics	Congress-person	§600	9 a.m.–3 p.m.	Town Car	0	0	4	3	3	2	9	-18	0	-25	0	-54	-18	-7
Pro Athlete	Superstar	§680	9 a.m.–4 p.m.	SUV	1	2	3	8	0	0	7	-18	0	-35	0	-65	-5	0
Science	Scholar	§640	10 a.m.–3 p.m.	Town Car	0	4	2	0	6	4	5	-18	0	-20	0	-48	-10	-10
Xtreme	Photo-journalist	§650	9 a.m.–3 p.m.	SUV	1	5	2	6	1	3	5	-18	0	-25	0	-54	-16	0

Requirements for Level 8 Positions

CAREER TRACK	POSITION	PAY	HOURS	CAR POOL VEHICLE	COOKING	REPAIR	CHARISMA	BODY	LOGIC	CREATIVITY	FAMILY/ FRIENDS	HUNGER	COMFORT	HYGIENE	BLADDER	ENERGY	FUN	SOCIAL
Business	President	§800	9 a.m.–5 p.m.	Town Car	0	2	5	2	6	3	10	-22	0	-30	0	-58	-19	0
Entertainment	Feature Star	§900	5 p.m.–1 a.m.	Limo	0	2	7	6	0	4	10	-22	0	-30	0	-58	-19	0
Law Enforcement	SWAT Team Leader	§625	9 a.m.–3 p.m.	Limo	1	4	3	6	5	1	8	-22	0	-30	0	-58	-19	0
Life of Crime	Counterfeiter	§760	9 p.m.–3 a.m.	Town Car	1	5	2	5	3	5	8	-22	0	-25	0	-58	-19	-15
Medicine	Surgeon	§700	10 p.m.–4 a.m.	Town Car	0	4	3	5	6	2	7	-22	0	-30	0	-58	-19	0
Military	Commander	§600	9 a.m.–3 p.m.	Military Jeep	1	6	5	5	5	0	5	-22	0	-33	0	-60	-25	0
Politics	Judge	§650	9 a.m.–3 p.m.	Town Car	0	0	5	4	4	3	11	-22	0	-30	0	-58	-22	-11
Pro Athlete	Assistant Coach	§850	9 a.m.–2 p.m.	SUV	2	2	4	9	0	1	9	-22	0	-40	0	-70	-6	0
Science	Top Secret Researcher	§740	10 a.m.–3 p.m.	Town Car	1	6	4	0	7	4	7	-22	0	-25	0	-52	-12	-13
Xtreme	Treasure Hunter	§725	10 a.m.–5 p.m.	SUV	1	6	3	7	3	4	7	-22	0	-34	0	-60	-15	-5

Requirements for Level 9 Positions

CAREER TRACK	POSITION	PAY	HOURS	CAR POOL VEHICLE	COOKING	REPAIR	CHARISMA	BODY	LOGIC	CREATIVITY	FAMILY/ FRIENDS	DAILY MOTIVE DECAY						
												HUNGER	COMFORT	HYGIENE	BLADDER	ENERGY	FUN	SOCIAL
Business	CEO	§950	9 a.m.–4 p.m.	Limo	0	2	6	2	7	5	12	-26	0	-35	0	-62	-22	0
Entertainment	Broadway Star	§1100	10 a.m.–5 p.m.	Limo	0	2	8	7	0	7	12	-26	0	-35	0	-62	-22	0
Law Enforcement	Police Chief	§650	9 a.m.–5 p.m.	Limo	1	4	4	7	7	3	10	-26	0	-35	0	-62	-22	0
Life of Crime	Smuggler	§900	9 a.m.–3 p.m.	Town Car	1	5	5	6	3	6	10	-26	0	-30	0	-62	-22	-20
Medicine	Medical Researcher	§775	9 p.m.–4 a.m.	Limo	0	5	4	6	8	3	9	-26	0	-35	0	-62	-22	0
Military	Astronaut	§625	9 a.m.–3 p.m.	Limo	1	9	5	8	6	0	6	-26	0	-35	0	-65	-30	0
Politics	Senator	§700	9 a.m.–6 p.m.	Limo	0	0	6	5	6	4	14	-26	0	-35	0	-62	-26	-15
Pro Athlete	Coach	§1,000	9 a.m.–3 p.m.	SUV	3	2	6	10	0	2	11	-26	0	-45	0	-75	-8	0
Science	Theorist	§870	10 a.m.–2 p.m.	Town Car	1	7	4	0	9	7	8	-26	0	-30	0	-56	-16	-16
Xtreme	Grand Prix Driver	§825	10 a.m.–4 p.m.	Bentley	1	6	5	7	5	7	9	-26	0	-35	0	-62	-5	-10

Requirements for Level 10 Positions

CAREER TRACK	POSITION	PAY	HOURS	CAR POOL VEHICLE	COOKING	REPAIR	CHARISMA	BODY	LOGIC	CREATIVITY	FAMILY/ FRIENDS	DAILY MOTIVE DECAY						
												HUNGER	COMFORT	HYGIENE	BLADDER	ENERGY	FUN	SOCIAL
Business	Business Tycoon	§1,200	9 a.m.–3 p.m.	Limo	0	2	8	2	9	6	14	-30	0	-40	0	-66	-25	0
Entertainment	Superstar	§1,400	10 a.m.–3 p.m.	Limo	0	2	10	8	0	10	14	-30	0	-40	0	-66	-25	0
Law Enforcement	Captain Hero	§700	10 a.m.–4 p.m.	Limo	1	4	6	7	10	5	12	-20	-80	-45	-25	-60	0	0
Life of Crime	Criminal Mastermind	§1,100	6 p.m.–12 a.m.	Limo	2	5	7	6	4	8	12	-30	0	-35	0	-66	-25	-25
Medicine	Chief of Staff	§850	9 p.m.–4 a.m.	Hospital Limo	0	6	6	7	9	4	11	-30	0	-40	0	-66	-25	0
Military	General	§650	9 a.m.–3 p.m.	Staff Sedan	1	10	7	10	9	0	8	-30	0	-40	0	-70	-35	0
Politics	Mayor	§750	9 a.m.–3 p.m	Limo	0	0	9	5	7	5	17	-30	0	-40	0	-66	-30	-20
Pro Athlete	Hall of Famer	§1,300	9 a.m.–3 p.m.	Limo	4	2	9	10	0	3	13	-30	0	-50	0	-80	-10	0
Science	Mad Scientist	§1,000	10 a.m.–2 p.m.	Limo	2	8	5	0	10	10	10	-30	0	-35	0	-60	-20	-20
Xtreme	International	§925	11 a.m.–5 p.m.	Bentley	2	6	8	8	6	9	11	-30	0	-30	0	-70	-20	-15

The Daily Grind

A working Sim needs to follow a schedule that is conducive to good job performance. Review the following tips as you devise a work schedule for your household.

Get Plenty of Sleep

Sims need to awake refreshed in order to arrive at work in a good mood. Send your Sims to bed early, and make sure there are no distractions (stereos, TVs, computers, etc.) that might interrupt their beauty sleep.

Fig. 4-6. That last set on the exercise bench paid off!

Fig. 4-5. Make sure your Sims get to bed early enough to restore maximum Energy before the alarm rings.

CAUTION

If two or more Sims in the house have jobs, the alarm clock rings for the earliest riser. Unfortunately, this wakes everyone else, regardless of when they have to be ready for the car pool. If you send the other Sims back to bed, you'll need to wake them manually, because the alarm clock only rings once each day.

Eat a Hearty Breakfast

When you're angling for a promotion, you need to arrive at work with all cylinders firing. When the alarm rings, send the designated house chef (the Sim with the highest Cooking Skill) to the kitchen to "Prepare a Meal." By the time your Sim is finished emptying his Bladder and completing necessary Hygiene, breakfast will be on the counter. There should be plenty of time to complete the meal and head to work with a full Hunger bar.

Set Your Alarm Clock

When set, the clock wakes your Sims two hours before the car pool arrives (one alarm clock takes care of the entire house). This is plenty of time to take care of Hunger, Bladder, and Hygiene Motive bars. If you still have time, improve your Sim's mood with a little non-strenuous fun like watching TV, or use the extra time to improve a Skill.

TIP

Make sure that your Sim is on the first floor and relatively close to the car pool within 15 minutes of departure to be sure he or she catches his or her ride. If you meet this deadline, your Sim will change clothes on the fly and sprint to the curb.

Make Friends and Influence Your Boss

Advancing through the first three levels does not carry a friendship requirement; however this ramps up very quickly. It helps to have a stay-at-home mate to concentrate on making friends. Remember that the career friendship requirement is for your household, not your Sim. So, if your mate or children have friends, they count toward your promotions, too.

Fig. 4-7. This Sim is just about out of Energy, but his Social score is maxed out and he's just made two new friends.

Take an Occasional Day Off to Recharge

If you find that your Sim is unable to have enough Fun or Social events to maintain a positive mood, skip a day of work and indulge. See a friend or two, work on Skills, or have some Fun. Just don't miss two days in a row or your Sim will be automatically fired!

Major Decisions

As you work your way up the career ladder, you encounter "major decisions" that involve various degrees of risk. They are winner-take-all, loser-gets-nada events that force you to gamble with your salary, integrity, or even your job. The following sections include a sample "major decision" for each career.

Business

Major decision: "Stock Option"

Player is given the choice of accepting a portfolio of company stock instead of salary for that pay period. The stock could double or tank. As a result, the player receives twice his salary or nothing at all for the pay period.

Entertainment

Major decision: "The Remake"

Your agent calls with an offer: Sim Studios wants you for the lead in a remake of *Citizen Kane*. Accepting will either send your Charisma sky high when the film succeeds wildly…or send it crashing if the turkey flops.

Law Enforcement

Major decision: "The Bribe"

A mobster you're investigating offers a huge bribe to drop the case. The charges won't stick without your testimony and you *could* suddenly "lose the evidence" and quietly pocket a nice nest egg…or get busted by Internal Affairs and have to start over on a new career track.

Life of Crime

Major decision: "The Perfect Crime"

You've just been handed a hot tip that an informant claims will be an easy knockover with loads of cash for the taking. Either the tip is gold, or it's a police sting. An arrest means your family is left at home alone while you're sent off to cool your heels in Sim City Prison for a while. If you succeed, your Charisma and Creativity Skills are enhanced.

Medicine

Major Decision: "Malpractice"

A former patient has slapped you with a massive malpractice suit. You can settle immediately by offering a payment equal to 50 percent of the cash in your household account. Or, take the bum to court. Lose, and all your furniture and household goods are repossessed. Win, and you receive a settlement equal to 100 percent of the cash in your household account.

Military

Major decision: "Gung Ho"

The general needs volunteers for a highly dangerous mission. You can refuse without penalty. If you accept, and succeed on the mission, you are decorated and immediately promoted to the next level. Failure means a demotion, soldier—you're broken down to the previous level.

Politics

Major decision: "Scandal"

An attractive young member of your team also happens to be heir to a fortune. He or she will finance your career advancement if you agree to "private consultations." You can refuse, with no change in status. Otherwise, there are two possible outcomes. You might get away with it and immediately advance *two* levels. If you're caught, you'll lose your friends when the scandal breaks in the media, and you'll be tossed from the career track to seek another.

Pro Athlete

Major Decision: "The Supermatch"

A one-on-one, pay-per-view contest pitting you against your greatest local rival is offered. If you win, it's worth double your paycheck. If you lose, the indignity comes complete with an injury costing you a reduction in your Body Skill along with a drop in Charisma. The player can always refuse at no penalty.

Science

Major decision: "The Experiment"

A science research firm is willing to pay you a fat bonus for conducting a complex experiment. However, the work must be conducted at your home, using rats as test subjects. Success means you collect the fee, with a bonus increase in your Logic Skill level. A failed experiment results in a dozen rats escaping into your home. That means a major bill from both your exterminator and your electrician (the rats have chewed through power cords.) Financial damage could be reduced if the Player's Repair Skills are strong.

Xtreme

Major decision: "Deep Freeze"

An arctic expedition is holding a spot open for you. It's a risky enterprise, so you may refuse. However, for a person in your particular line of work, that refusal will lower your Charisma. If you join the team, and they reach their goal, you will be rewarded with a considerable rise in Charisma. If the mission goes awry, your Sim is "lost on an iceberg" for a period of game time.

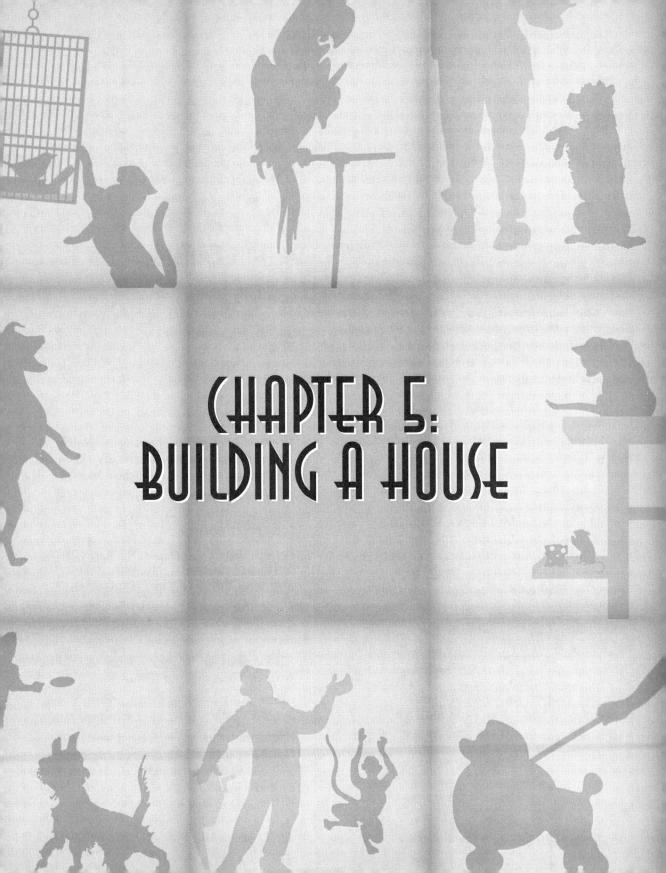

CHAPTER 5:
BUILDING A HOUSE

Introduction

Anyone who has ever built a home knows that the best laid plans of architects can sometimes turn into a house of horrors when the walls start going up. The same holds true in *The Sims*, where you have enough power to build a magnificent dream house or your worst residential nightmare. Limited only by your bank account, you can build a conservative dwelling that is functional above all else, or you can drop a family of eight in the middle of a meadow with only a bathroom and a refrigerator. It's all possible in *The Sims*, but rest assured that your family will deliver a quick—and sometimes scathing—critique when the clock starts ticking on their simulated lives.

In this chapter, we take you through the house design process from terrain preparation to landscaping. For demonstration purposes, we will use just about every building option available. Obviously, you would need a pile of Simoleans to do this in the game. However, we also cover important design considerations that enable you to maximize your Room score, regardless of your budget. In this chapter, we limit our discussion to the available options in Build Mode only. For detailed descriptions of more than 150 *Sims* objects, see the next chapter.

Of course, our suggestions are just the beginning. Sims thrive on the individuality of their creator, and if you want to build dungeons, sprawling compounds, or one-room huts, you have our support and encouragement. Remember, a bad house is no match for the bulldozer—your next house is only a click away!

TIP

Don't try to build your dream house at the beginning of the game. It's easier to tear down your original house and start over after you've fattened up your bank account.

Design Considerations

Before we introduce you to the various options available in Build Mode, here is a checklist for your basic floor plan. Invariably, your unique family of Sims will make their needs known to you as the game progresses. However, if you follow these house design basics, you should get your family off to a positive start with a minimum of emotional outbursts.

* **Don't worry about having room to expand. Build your first house to match the number of Sims in your family.**
* **Keep the bathroom centrally located. A door on either side allows quick access for emergencies.**
* **If you start with three Sims or more, build one or more half-bathrooms (toilet and sink only) to ease the crunch.**
* **Place the house close to the street, so you don't have to do the hundred yard dash to meet your car pool.**
* **Allow enough open wall for your kitchen countertops and appliances.**
* **Make your kitchen large enough to accommodate a small table and chairs.**
* **If you don't want a separate den or family room, make one of the bedrooms large enough to handle a computer desk and chair.**

Terrain Tools

In most locations, you can build a roomy house on a flat piece of land without having to level the terrain. However, if you want to build a house near the water or at the edge of a hill, you'll need to smooth the sloping tiles before building a wall, as displayed in figure 5-1.

Fig. 5-1. You can't place a wall section until you smooth the slope.

The Terrain Tool (shovel icon) can be a little tricky to master. On level ground, you can place the shovel at any intersection of horizontal and vertical grid lines, and then click to level, lower, or raise the tile. However, sometimes, due to extreme depth or elevation (usually at the edge of a gully or alongside water), you can't access this intersecting point. When this occurs, you receive a message telling you that the tile cannot be modified (figure 5-2).

TIP

The grid lines become noticeably darker when a previously elevated or lowered tile becomes level.

Fig. 5-2. You cannot level a tile at the water's edge.

In most cases, there is no need to edit the terrain, unless you want to add a sunken hot tub or drop an outdoor play set into a pit. Remember that you must level the ground in the pit before you can place an object (see figure 5-3).

Fig. 5-3. You cannot place the play set until the tiles in the pit are level.

Wall and Fence Tools

There are several tools here, but your first step is to "frame" your house. Simply place the cursor at any tile intersection. Then click, hold, and drag to place your wall (figure 5-4). When you release the mouse button, the wood framing will change to the type of wall you selected on the Control Panel (see page 52 for descriptions of wall types).

Fig. 5-4. Drag and release to place a wall.

Although you must start a wall at an intersection, you are not limited to square walls. Simply drag the cursor at an angle to create an interesting corner (figure 5-5). However, don't make the angled walls too long. You cannot place doors, windows, or objects on these walls. Also, you cannot connect an angled wall to an existing straight wall inside your house.

Fig. 5-5. Angled corners help you transform a boring box into a custom home.

Wall Tool

Wall Types

NAME	COST (PER SECTION)	DESCRIPTION
White Picket Fence	§10	Outdoor fencing
Privacy Fence	§35	8-foot outdoor fence
Monticello Balustrade	§45	Railings for balconies and stairs
Wrought Iron Balustrade	§45	Railings for balconies and stairs
Tumbleweed Wooden Column	§70	Support columns for second stories or patio covers
Wall Tool	§70	Basic unfinished wall
The Zorba Ionic Column	§80	Classic, white Graeco-Roman column
Chester Brick Column	§100	All brick, squared off column

Door and Window Tools

Door Tool

Sims are very active. They seek the best path for their current task, and they think nothing of going out one exterior door and back in through another, if it's the best route. The least expensive Walnut Door (figure 5-6) is only §100, but because it is solid, your Room score does not benefit from outside light. If at all possible, invest in one of the windowed doors, and ideally, pick the multi-paned Monticello Door for maximum light.

Fig. 5-6. The Walnut Door gives your Sims privacy, but it doesn't allow outside light to improve your Room score.

Door Types

NAME	COST	NOTES
Walnut Door	§100	Solid door without windows
Maple Door Frame	§150	Wooden door frame for rooms that do not require total privacy
Federal Lattice Window Door	§200	Glass panes in the upper half of door
Windsor Door	§300	Designer leaded glass door
Monticello Door	§400	7 rows of 3 panes, topped with a 6-pane half circle, allow maximum light to flow into your home

Window Tool

Let the sun shine in to pump up your Room score. Sims love light, so install plenty of windows from the start. Simply click on the selected window and place it on any right-angle wall (remember, you cannot place doors, windows, or objects on a diagonal wall). Window style is strictly personal—all windows exert the same positive effect on the Room score.

TIP

For aesthetic value, match your windows to your door style, such as the Monticello Door with Monticello Windows, as pictured in figure 5-7.

Fig. 5-7. Monticello Doors and Windows provide maximum light.

Window Types

NAME	COST	DESCRIPTION
Single-Pane Fixed Window	§50	This economy window still lets in the sun.
Single-Hung Window	§55	This looks good over the kitchen sink.
Privacy Window	§60	Tired of the neighborhood peeping Toms? This window is positioned higher on the wall.
Plate Glass Window	§65	This one's strictly glass from floor to ceiling.
El Sol Window	§80	This round ornamental window is a nice change from square and rectangular styles.
Monticello Window	§110	Use as a bedroom window to complement the Monticello door.
Windsor Window	§120	This ornamental natural wood window adds turn-of-the-century character to your home.
Monticello Window Full-Length	§200	This dramatic window looks beautiful on either side of a Monticello door.

Floor Tool

Unless you like grass in your living room, use the Floor Tool to lay some flooring inside your house. *The Sims* also includes outdoor flooring that works well in patios, backyard barbecue areas, or as pathways to a pool or play area. One tile covers a single grid, and you can quickly finish an entire room with a single shift-click. The price range for floor coverings is §10–§20, and you have a selection of 29 different styles/colors.

TIP

When you lay flooring inside a room with angled walls, half of the floor tiles appear on the other side of the wall, in another room or outside the house (see figure 5-8). To remove these outside tiles, place any floor type over the tiles, hold down the Ctrl *key, and then click to delete them. The flooring on the other side of the wall remains undisturbed.*

Fig. 5-8. After you finish the inside flooring, go back and delete the external tiles.

NOTE

You can use any type of flooring inside or outside.

Flooring Types

- **Carpeting (7)**
- **Cement (1)**
- **Ceramic Tile-Small Tiles (3)**
- **Checkerboard Linoleum (1)**
- **Clay Paver Tiles (1)**
- **Colored Pavement (1)**
- **Granite (2)**
- **Gravel (1)**
- **Hardwood Plank (1)**
- **Inlaid Hardwood (1)**
- **Italian Tile (1)**
- **Poured Concrete (1)**
- **Shale (1)**
- **Striped Pavement (2, Both Directions)**
- **Tatami Mats (2)**
- **Terracotta Tile (1)**
- **Wood Parquet (2)**

Wallpaper Tool

Fig. 5-9. Use the Wallpaper Tool to create a different mood in every room.

There are 30 different indoor/outdoor wall coverings in *The Sims,* and just as with floor coverings, you are limited only by your budget and sense of style. Prices range from §4 for basic wallpaper to §14 for granite block. If you change your mind after putting up the wallpaper, you can rip it down and get your money back by holding down the Ctrl key and clicking on the ugly panel.

Wallpaper Types

- **Adobe (1)**
- **Aluminum Siding (1)**
- **Brick (2)**
- **Granite (1)**
- **Interior Wall Treatments (6 Fabric and Paint Combinations)**
- **Japanese Paper/Screens (4)**
- **Paint (4)**
- **Plaster (1)**
- **Stucco (1)**
- **Tudor (1)**
- **Wainscoting (1)**
- **Wallpaper (4)**
- **Wood Clapboard (1)**
- **Wood Paneling (1)**
- **Wood Shingles (1)**

Stair Tool

You may not plan to build a second story immediately, but it's still a good idea to place your staircase before you start filling your house with objects. Choose from four staircases, two at §900 and two at §1,200. But, no matter how much you spend, they still get your Sims up and down the same way.

Style is considerably less important than function. You don't want to interrupt the traffic flow inside your house, especially to critical rooms such as the bathroom and kitchen. For this reason, staircases work well against a wall, where they are out of the way, or between two large, open rooms, such as the kitchen and family room (figure 5-10).

Fig. 5-10. Both of these placements keep the staircases out of the main traffic patterns.

If you don't have the money to finish the second story, just place the staircase and forget about it. The Sims won't go upstairs until you add a second story. After the staircase is positioned, the process for building a second story is exactly the same as building the first floor. The only obvious difference is that the buildable wall space extends out one square beyond the walls on the first floor. This allows you to squeeze a little extra space for a larger room or balcony.

Roof Tool

Although it is much easier to play *The Sims* using the Walls Cutaway or Walls Down options on the Control Panel, you will want to step back and enjoy your masterpiece in all of its crowning glory. The Roof Tool allows you to select a Shallow, Medium, or Steep Pitch for your roof, and choose from a selection of four roof patterns.

Fig. 5-11. Our house has a Steep Pitch with dark roof tiles.

Water Tools

Now that you have walls, floors, and doors, it's time to add a pool. Of course, this isn't a necessity, but your Sims love to swim, and it's an easy way to add important Body points. After placing your pool, don't forget to add a diving board so your Sims can get in, and a ladder so they can climb out. As you build your pool, the Water Tool places light-colored cement squares as decking. You can go back and cover these tiles with the outdoor surface of your choice, as displayed in figure 5-12. You can also add fencing around your deck to give your pool a more finished look.

Fig. 5-12. With the pool and decking in place, you have room to add an outdoor barbecue and beverage cart.

Fireplace Tool

Fig. 5-13. It looks innocent enough, but a roaring fire can turn nearby objects or Sims into a deadly inferno.

When placed safely out of the way of flammable objects, a fireplace adds a major boost to the Room score. However, it can be a dangerous fire hazard if Sims wander too close, so give it a wide berth when a fire is roaring.

Plant Tool

Now, it's time to put the finishing touches on the exterior of your house. Using the Plant Tool, you can select from 14 different plants, priced from §5 for Wildflowers to §300 for an Apple Tree. The following types of vegetation are included:

Plant Types

• **Flowers (4)**
• **Bushes (1)**
• **Hedges (2)**
• **Shrubs (2)**
• **Trees (5)**

Let your green thumb go wild, but don't forget that only trees and shrubs will thrive without regular watering. If you want colorful flowers, you'll probably need to hire a Gardener.

Fig. 5-14. This colorful landscaping will require the services of a Gardener, or a Sim with a lot of time to kill.

Special Editing Tools

In addition to the building tools described above, there are two other options on the Build Mode Control Panel. The curved arrows pictured at the bottom corner of figure 5-15 allow you to undo or repeat your last action(s). This is a quick way to delete unwanted items.

Fig. 5-15. Click Undo Last to reverse your most recent actions.

If the undo button is unavailable, you can click on the Hand Tool, select any object, and then press the Delete key to sell it back. For directions on how to delete walls, wall coverings, and floor coverings, see the appropriate sections in this chapter.

Fig. 5-16. Select an item with the Hand Tool, then press Delete to make it go away.

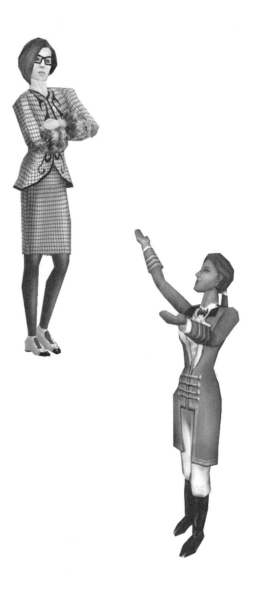

CHAPTER 6:
MATERIAL SIMS

Introduction

This chapter covers the eight categories of objects available in Buy Mode: Seating, Surfaces, Decorative, Electronics, Appliances, Plumbing, Lighting, and Miscellaneous. Every object is listed with its purchase price, related Motives, and Efficiency ratings. You can shop 'til you drop, but it's more important to buy smart than to buy often. Our comprehensive Buying Guide is just ahead, but first let's study some important factors that impact your spending habits.

Buying for Needs, Instead of Needing to Buy

If you select a ready-made house for your new Sim family, you acquire walls, floors, and a roof, but little else. The house is empty, with nary a toilet, bed, or refrigerator in sight. Depending upon how much you spent on the house, you'll have a few thousand Simoleans to use in Buy Mode, where you can purchase more than 150 objects. Most objects affect your Sims' environment in positive ways. However, not every object is a necessity. In fact, if you are a recovering shopping channel addict, this is not a good time to fall off your wallet. Make your first purchases with The Sims' Motives (or Needs) in mind. You can review your Sims' current Needs state by clicking on the Mood icon. We provide detailed descriptions in the Motives chapter, but for now, here is a basic shopping list that will help you get your Sims' Need bars out of the red zone during the early stages of a game.

Fig. 6-1. Despite logging only five hours of sleep, Bella is feeling pretty good, thanks to her §3000 Mission bed.

Fig. 6-2. A big-screen TV is fun for your Sims, but also for the neighbors, who will often hang out, and boost your Social score.

NEED	ITEM	EXPLANATION
Hunger	Refrigerator, Food Processor, Stove	A refrigerator alone will sustain life, but you will greatly improve the quality of Sim meals by using a food processor and stove. However, there is a risk of fire if your Sim doesn't have at least two Cooking Skill points.
Comfort	Bed, Chairs	Sims will sleep anywhere when they are tired, but a bed is highly recommended for sleeping, and you'll need chairs (for eating and working at the computer), and a couch for napping. A bathtub provides a little extra comfort for your Sims, but it isn't critical, provided you have a shower.
Hygiene	Sink, Shower	Dirty Sims spend a lot of time waving their arms in the air to disperse their body odor. Not a pretty sight. Fortunately, a sink and shower go a long way toward improving their state of mind (not to mention the smell).
Bladder	Toilet	When you gotta go, you gotta go. Sims prefer using a toilet, but if one is not available, they will relieve themselves on the floor. This not only causes great shame and embarrassment, but someone in your family will have to clean up the mess. It's also very bad for your Hygiene levels.
Energy	Bed	If you don't want to spawn a family of insomniacs, buy a sufficient number of beds for your Sims. A shot of coffee or espresso provides a temporary Energy boost, but it is definitely not a long-term solution.
Fun	TV	The boob tube is the easiest and cheapest way to give your Sims a break from their daily grinds. You can add other, more exciting, items later, but this is your best choice early on.
Social	Telephone	Ignore this for a short time while you focus on setting up your house. However, don't force your Sims into a solitary lifestyle. Other Sims may walk by the house, but you'll have better results after buying a telephone, so that you can invite people over and gain Social points when they arrive.
Room	Windows, Lamps, Decorations, Landscaping	Sims like plenty of light, from windows during the day and artificial lighting at night. Table Lamps are the cheapest, but they can only be placed on raised surfaces. As your game progresses, you can add decorations and landscaping to boost the Room score.

Sims Can Be Hard to Please

Given a fat bank account, it would seem that you can always cheer up your Sims with a few expensive purchases. Not exactly. While you are spending your hard-earned Simoleans, the Sims are busy comparing everything that you buy to everything they already own. If you fail to keep your Sims in the manner to which they are accustomed, their responses to your new objects may be indifferent or even downright negative. Every time you make a purchase, the game uses an assessment formula to calculate your Sim's response. The logic goes like this:

Fig. 6-3. Compared to the §2,100 "Snails With Icicles in Nose," this §45 clown picture doesn't quite stack up.

Your Diminishing Net Worth

When times are tough, you may need to raise cash by selling objects in your house. With rare exception, you will never match your initial investment, thanks to instant depreciation, and as time goes on, your belongings continue to lose value until they reach their depreciation limits. The following table lists every object in *The Sims* (alphabetically), including purchase price and depreciated values.

- **Calculates the average value of everything in your house (including outdoor items).**

- **Subtracts 10 percent of the new object's value for each existing copy of the same item. Don't expect your family members to jump for joy if you add a hot tub to every room in the house.**

- **Compares the value of the new object with all existing objects in your house. If the new purchase is worth 20 percent or more above the average value of current items, the Sim exhibits a positive response by clapping.**

- **If the new object is within 20 percent (above or below) of the current average value of all items in your household, the Sim gives you an uninspired shrug.**

- **If the new object is less than 20 percent below the average value, your Sim waves it off and you'll see a red X through the object.**

TIP

Although depreciation reduces the value of your furnishings over time, there is a buyer's remorse period when you can return the item for full value (if it has been less than 24 hours since you purchased it). So, if you have second thoughts about that new hot tub, simply select the item and hit the Delete key to get your money back.

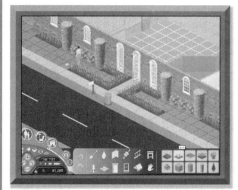

Fig. 6-4. This Pyrotorre Gas Range is §1,000 new, but after depreciation it's worth only §790.

Object Depreciation

NAME	PURCHASE PRICE	INITIAL DEPRECIATION	DAILY DEPRECIATION	DEPRECIATION LIMIT
Alarm: Burglar	§250	§62	§2	§50
Alarm: Smoke	§50	§12	§0	§10
Aquarium	§200	§30	§2	§80
Bar	§800	§120	§8	§320
Barbecue	§350	§70	§4	§105
Basketball Hoop (Cheap Eaze)	§650	§98	§6	§260
Bed: Double	§450	§68	§4	§180
Bed: Double (Mission)	§3,000	§450	§30	§1,200
Bed: Double (Napoleon)	§1,000	§150	§10	§400
Bed: Single (Spartan)	§300	§45	§3	§120
Bed: Single (Tyke Nyte)	§450	§68	§4	§180
Bench: Garden	§250	§38	§2	§100
Bookshelf: Amishim	§500	§75	§5	§200
Bookshelf: Libri di Regina	§900	§135	§9	§360
Bookshelf: Pine	§250	§38	§2	§100
Chair: Deck (Survivall)	§150	§22	§2	§60
Chair: Dining (Empress)	§600	§90	§6	§240
Chair: Dining (Parisienne)	§1,200	§180	§12	§480
Chair: Dining (Teak)	§200	§30	§2	§80
Chair: Dining (Werkbunnst)	§80	§12	§1	§32
Chair: Living Room (Citronel)	§450	§68	§4	§180
Chair: Living Room (Country Class)	§250	§38	§2	§100
Chair: Living Room (Sarrbach)	§500	§75	§5	§200
Chair: Living Room (Wicker)	§80	§12	§1	§32
Chair: Office	§100	§15	§1	§40

NAME	PURCHASE PRICE	INITIAL DEPRECIATION	DAILY DEPRECIATION	DEPRECIATION LIMIT
Chair: Recliner (Back Slack)	§250	§38	§2	§100
Chair: Recliner (Von Braun)	§850	§128	§8	§340
Chess Set	§500	§75	§5	§200
Clock: Alarm	§30	§4	§0	§12
Clock: Grandfather	§3,500	§525	§35	§1,400
Coffee: Espresso Machine	§450	§90	§4	§135
Coffeemaker	§85	§17	§1	§26
Computer (Brahma 2000)	§2,800	§700	§28	§560
Computer (Marco)	§6,500	§1,625	§65	§1,300
Computer (Microscotch)	§1,800	§450	§18	§360
Computer (Moneywell)	§999	§250	§10	§200
Counter: Bath (Count Blanc)	§400	§60	§4	§160
Counter: Kitchen (Barcelona: In)	§800	§120	§8	§320
Counter: Kitchen (Barcelona: Out)	§800	§120	§8	§320
Counter: Kitchen (NuMica)	§150	§22	§2	§60
Counter: Kitchen (Tiled)	§250	§38	§2	§100
Desk (Cupertino)	§220	§33	§2	§88
Desk (Mesquite)	§80	§12	§1	§32
Desk (Redmond)	§800	§120	§8	§320
Dishwasher (Dish Duster)	§550	§110	§6	§165
Dishwasher (Fuzzy Logic)	§950	§190	§10	§285
Dollhouse	§180	§27	§2	§72
Dresser (Antique Armoire)	§1,200	§180	§12	§480
Dresser (Kinderstuff)	§300	§45	§3	§120

NAME	PURCHASE PRICE	INITIAL DEPRECIATION	DAILY DEPRECIATION	DEPRECIATION LIMIT
Dresser (Oak Armoire)	§550	§82	§6	§220
Dresser (Pinegulcher)	§250	§38	§2	§100
Easel	§250	§38	§2	§100
Exercise Machine	§700	§105	§7	§280
Flamingo	§12	§2	§0	§5
Food Processor	§220	§44	§2	§66
Fountain	§700	§105	§7	§280
Fridge (Freeze Secret)	§2,500	§500	§25	§750
Fridge (Llamark)	§600	§120	§6	§180
Fridge (Porcina)	§1,200	§240*	§12	§360
Hot Tub	§6,500	§1,300	§65	§1,950
Lamp: Floor (Halogen)	§50	§8	§0	§20
Lamp: Floor (Lumpen)	§100	§15	§1	§40
Lamp: Floor (Torchosteronne)	§350	§52	§4	§140
Lamp: Garden	§50	§7	§1	§20
Lamp: Love n' Haight Lava	§80	§12	§1	§32
Lamp: Table (Antique)	§300	§45	§3	§120
Lamp: Table (Bottle)	§25	§4	§0	§10
Lamp: Table (Ceramiche)	§85	§13	§1	§34
Lamp: Table (Elite)	§180	§27	§2	§72
Medicine Cabinet	§125	§19	§1	§50
Microwave	§250	§50	§2	§75
Mirror: Floor	§150	§22	§2	§60
Mirror: Wall	§100	§15	§1	§40
Phone: Tabletop	§50	§12	§0	§10
Phone: Wall	§75	§19	§1	§15
Piano	§3,500	§525	§35	§1,400
Pinball Machine	§1,800	§450	§18	§360
Plant: Big (Cactus)	§150	§22	§2	§60
Plant: Big (Jade)	§160	§24	§2	§64
Plant: Big (Rubber)	§120	§18	§1	§48

NAME	PURCHASE PRICE	INITIAL DEPRECIATION	DAILY DEPRECIATION	DEPRECIATION LIMIT
Plant: Small (Geranium)	§45	§7	§0	§18
Plant: Small (Spider)	§35	§5	§0	§14
Plant: Small (Violets)	§30	§4	§0	§12
Play Structure	§1,200	§180	§12	§480
Pool Table	§4,200	§630	§42	§1,680
Shower	§650	§130	§6	§195
Sink: Bathroom Pedestal	§400	§80	§4	§120
Sink: Kitchen (Double)	§500	§100	§5	§150
Sink: Kitchen (Single)	§250	§50	§2	§75
Sofa (Blue Pinstripe)	§400	§60	§4	§160
Sofa (Contempto)	§200	§30	§2	§80
Sofa (Country)	§450	§68	§4	§180
Sofa (Deiter)	§1,100	§165	§11	§440
Sofa (Dolce)	§1,450	§218	§14	§580
Sofa (Recycled)	§180	§27	§2	§72
Sofa (SimSafari)	§220	§33	§2	§88
Sofa: Loveseat (Blue Pinstripe)	§360	§54	§4	§144
Sofa: Loveseat (Contempto)	§150	§22	§2	§60
Sofa: Loveseat (Country)	§340	§51	§3	§136
Sofa: Loveseat (Indoor-Outdoor)	§160	§24	§2	§64
Sofa: Loveseat (Luxuriare)	§875	§131	§9	§350
Stereo (Strings)	§2,550	§638	§26	§510
Stereo (Zimantz)	§650	§162	§6	§130
Stereo: Boom Box	§100	§25	§1	§20
Stove (Dialectric)	§400	§80	§4	§120
Stove (Pyrotorre)	§1,000	§200	§10	§300
Table: Dining (Colonial)	§200	§30	§2	§80
Table: Dining (Mesa)	§450	§68	§4	§180

NAME	PURCHASE PRICE	INITIAL DEPRECIATION	DAILY DEPRECIATION	DEPRECIATION LIMIT
Table: Dining (NuMica)	§95	§14	§1	§38
Table: Dining (Parisienne)	§1,200	§180	§12	§480
Table: End (Anywhere)	§120	§18	§1	§48
Table: End (Imperious)	§135	§20	§1	§54
Table: End (KinderStuff)	§75	§11	§1	§30
Table: End (Mission)	§250	§38	§2	§100
Table: End (Pinegulcher)	§40	§6	§0	§16
Table: End (Sumpto)	§300	§45	§3	§120
Table: End (Wicker)	§55	§8	§1	§22
Table: Outdoor (Backwoods)	§200	§30	§2	§80
Toaster Oven	§100	§20	§1	§30
Toilet (Flush Force)	§1,200	§240	§12	§360
Toilet (Hygeia-O-Matic)	§300	§60	§3	§90
Tombstone/Urn	§5	§1	§0	§2
Toy Box	§50	§8	§0	§20
Train Set: Large	§955	§239	§10	§191
Train Set: Small	§80	§20	§1	§16
Trash Compactor	§375	§75	§4	§112
Tub (Hydrothera)	§3,200	§640	§32	§960
Tub (Justa)	§800	§160	§8	§240
Tub (Sani-Queen)	§1,500	§300	§15	§450
TV (Monochrome)	§85	§21	§1	§17
TV (Soma)	§3,500	§875	§35	§700
TV (Trottco)	§500	§125	§5	§100
VR Glasses	§2,300	§575	§23	§460

The Sims Buying Guide

The following sections represent the eight item categories that appear when you click the Buy Mode button on the control panel. We've added a few subcategories to make it easier to find a specific object. The Efficiency Value (1–10) indicates how well the item satisfies each Motive. You get what you pay for in *The Sims*, so an §80 chair doesn't quite stack up to an §850 recliner when it comes to boosting your Comfort level, and it cannot restore Energy.

Seating

Chairs

There are three types of chairs in *The Sims*: movable, stationary, and reclining. Any chair will function at a desk or table for eating and using objects. If your budget is tight, you can also use cheaper chairs for watching TV or reading, but their Comfort ratings are very low. You can use high-ticket dining room chairs at the computer, but that is probably overkill. You are better off placing them in the dining room where you receive greater benefit from their enhanced Room ratings.

Stationary chairs are cushier and nicely upholstered (depending on your taste, of course), and they usually provide more comfort. Finally, the reclining chairs are top of the line, giving you increased comfort and the added benefit of being able to catch a few Zs in the reclining position.

TIP

Chair placement is critical, especially around tables. A Sim will not move a chair sideways, only forward and backward. So, position the chair properly or the Sim will not be able to use the table (or what is on it). Also, be careful not to trap a Sim in a corner when a chair is pulled out. For example, if a child is playing with a train set in the corner of the room, and another Sim pulls out a chair to use the computer, the child would be trapped in the corner until the computer user is finished.

Werkbunnst All-Purpose Chair

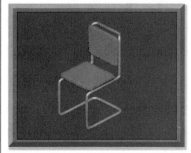

Type: Movable

Cost: §80

Motive: Comfort (2)

Posture Plus Office Chair

Type: Movable

Cost: §100

Motive: Comfort (3)

Deck Chair by Survivall

Type: Movable

Cost: §150

Motive: Comfort (3)

Parisienne Dining Chair

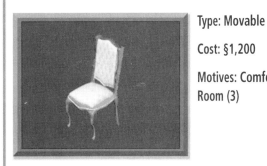

Type: Movable

Cost: §1,200

Motives: Comfort (6), Room (3)

Touch of Teak Dinette Chair

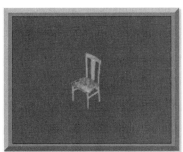

Type: Movable

Cost: §200

Motive: Comfort (3)

Sioux City Wicker Chair

Type: Stationary

Cost: §80

Motive: Comfort (2)

Empress Dining Room Chair

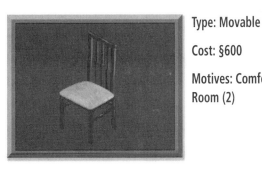

Type: Movable

Cost: §600

Motives: Comfort (4), Room (2)

Country Class Armchair

Type: Stationary

Cost: §250

Motive: Comfort (4)

"Citronel" from Chiclettina Inc.

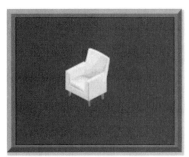

Type: Stationary

Cost: §450

Motive: Comfort (6)

"The Sarrbach" by Werkbunnst

Type: Stationary

Cost: §500

Motive: Comfort (6)

"Back Slack" Recliner

Type: Recliner

Cost: §250

Motives: Comfort (6),
Energy (3)

"Von Braun" Recliner

Type: Recliner

Cost: §850

Motives: Comfort (9),
Energy (3)

Couches

Sitting down is fine for reading, eating, or working, but for serious vegging, your Sims need a good couch. When selecting a couch, function is more important than quality. If you are looking for a place to take naps, pay more attention to the Energy rating than the Comfort or Room ratings. A multipurpose couch should have good Energy and Comfort ratings. However, if you are furnishing your party area, select one that looks good, thereby enhancing your Room rating. Stay away from the cheapest couches (under §200). For a few extra dollars, a medium-priced couch will make your Sims a lot happier. When you're flush with Simoleans, don't forget to dress up your garden with the outdoor bench. You can't sleep on it, but it looks great.

Contempto Loveseat

Cost: §150

Motives: Comfort (3),
Energy (4)

Indoor-Outdoor Loveseat

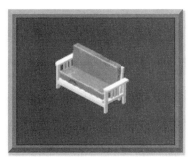

Cost: §160

Motives: Comfort (3), Energy (4)

SimSafari Sofa

Cost: §220

Motives: Comfort (3), Energy (5)

Recycled Couch

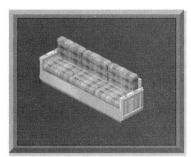

Cost: §180

Motives: Comfort (2), Energy (5)

Parque Fresco del Aire Bench

Cost: §250

Motive: Comfort (2)

Contempto Couch

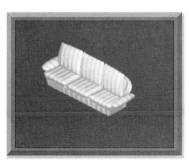

Cost: §200

Motives: Comfort (3), Energy (5)

Country Class Loveseat

Cost: §340

Motives: Comfort (5), Energy (4)

Pinstripe Loveseat from Zecutime

Cost: §360

Motives: Comfort (5), Energy (4)

Luxuriare Loveseat

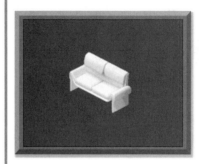

Cost: §875

Motives: Comfort (8), Energy (4), Room (2)

Pinstripe Sofa from Zecutime

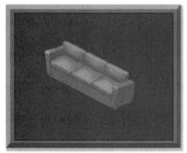

Cost: §400

Motives: Comfort (5), Energy (5)

"The Deiter" by Werkbunnst

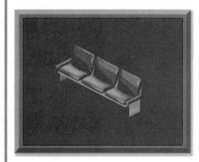

Cost: §1,100

Motives: Comfort (8), Energy (5), Room (3)

Country Class Sofa

Cost: §450

Motives: Comfort (5), Energy (5)

Dolce Tutti Frutti Sofa

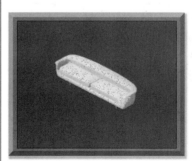

Cost: §1,450

Motives: Comfort (9), Energy (5), Room (3)

Beds

Getting enough sleep can be one of the most frustrating goals in *The Sims*, especially if there is a new baby in the house, or your car pool arrives at some ungodly hour of the morning. In the early stages of a game, it is not important to spend a bundle of money on a designer bed. However, an upgrade later on is well worth the money, because a top-of-the-line bed recharges your Energy bar faster.

Tyke Nyte Bed

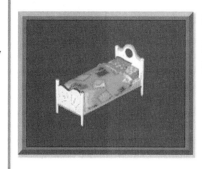

Cost: §450

Motives: Comfort (7), Energy (7)

Spartan Special

Cost: §300

Motives: Comfort (6), Energy (7)

Napoleon Sleigh Bed

Cost: §1,000

Motives: Comfort (8), Energy (9)

Cheap Eazzzzze Double Sleeper

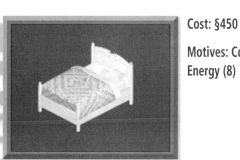

Cost: §450

Motives: Comfort (7), Energy (8)

Modern Mission Bed

Cost: §3,000

Motives: Comfort (9), Energy (10), Room (3)

Surfaces

Sims will eat or read standing up if they have to, but they won't be particularly happy about it. Sitting at a table while eating a meal bolsters a Sim's Comfort. Since your Sims have to eat to satisfy Hunger, they might as well improve Comfort, too. Many objects require elevated surfaces, so allow enough room for nightstands (alarm clock, lamps), tables (computer), and countertops (microwave, coffeemaker, etc.), when you design the interior of your house. Also, your Sims cannot prepare food on a table, so provide ample countertop space in the kitchen, or you may find them wandering into the bathroom to chop veggies on the counter (hair in the soup—yummy!).

Countertops

NuMica Kitchen Counter

Cost: §150

Motive: None

Tiled Counter

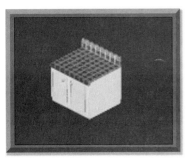

Cost: §250

Motive: None

Count Blanc Bathroom Counter

Cost: §400

Motive: None

"Barcelona" Outcurve Counter

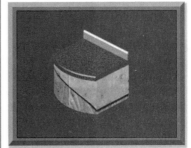

Cost: §800

Motive: Room (2)

"Barcelona" Incurve Counter

Cost: §800

Motive: Room (2)

End Tables

Pinegulcher End Table

Cost: §40

Motive: None

Wicker Breeze End Table

Cost: §55

Motive: None

"Anywhere" End Table

Cost: §120

Motive: None

Imperious Island End Table

Cost: §135

Motive: None

Modern Mission End Table

Cost: §250

Motive: Room (1)

Sumpto End Table

Cost: §300

Motive: Room (1)

KinderStuff Nightstand

Cost: §75

Motive: None

Desks/Tables

Mesquite Desk/Table

Cost: §80

Motive: None

NuMica Folding Card Table

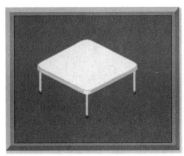

Cost: §95

Motive: None

"Colonial Legacy" Dining Table

Cost: §200

Motive: None

Backwoods Table by Survivall

Cost: §200

Motive: None

London "Cupertino" Collection Desk/Table

Cost: §220

Motive: None

London "Mesa" Dining Design

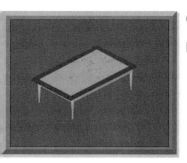

Cost: §450

Motive: Room (2)

The "Redmond" Desk/Table

Cost: §800

Motive: Room (2)

Parisienne Dining Table

Cost: §1,200

Motive: Room (3)

Decorative

After the essential furnishings are in place, you can improve your Room score by adding decorative objects. Some items, such as the grandfather clock and aquarium, require regular maintenance, but most decorative items exist solely for your Sims' viewing pleasure. You might even get lucky and buy a painting or sculpture that increases in value. In addition to enhancing the Room score, the aquarium and fountain have Fun value.

Pink Flamingo

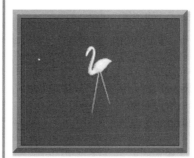

Cost: §12

Motive: Room (2)

African Violet

Cost: §30

Motive: Room (1)

Spider Plant

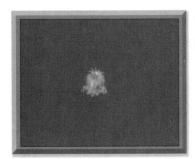

Cost: §35

Motive: Room (1)

Watercolor by J.M.E.

Cost: §75

Motive: Room (1)

"Roxana" Geranium

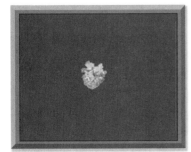

Cost: §45

Motive: Room (1)

Rubber Tree Plant

Cost: §120

Motive: Room (2)

"Tragic Clown" Painting

Cost: §45

Motive: Room (1)

Echinopsis maximus Cactus

Cost: §150

Motive: Room (2)

Jade Plant

Cost: §160

Motive: Room (2)

"Delusion de Grandeur"

Cost: §360

Motive: Room (2)

Poseidon's Adventure Aquarium

Cost: §200

Motive: Fun (1), Room (2)

"Fountain of Tranquility"

Cost: §700

Motives: Fun (1), Room (2)

"Bi-Polar" by Conner I.N.

Cost: §240

Motive: Room (2)

Landscape #12,001 by Manny Kopees

Cost: §750

Motive: Room (3)

Bust of Athena by Klassick Repro. Inc.

Cost: §875

Motive: Room (3)

Portrait Grid by Payne A. Pitcher

Cost: §3,200

Motive: Room (8)

"Scylla and Charybdis"

Cost: §1,450

Motive: Room (4)

Grandfather Clock

Cost: §3,500

Motive: Room (7)

Snails With Icicles in Nose

Cost: §2,140

Motive: Room (5)

Blue China Vase

Cost: §4,260

Motive: Room (7)

"Still Life, Drapery and Crumbs"

Cost: §7,600

Motive: Room (9)

"Large Black Slab" by ChiChi Smith

Cost: §12,648

Motive: Room (10)

Electronics

This game offers a veritable potpourri of high-tech gadgetry, ranging from potentially lifesaving items such as smoke detectors to nonessential purchases such as pinball games or virtual reality headsets. Beyond the critical electronics items—smoke detectors, telephone for receiving calls or calling services and friends, TV for cheap fun, and computer for finding a job—you should focus on items with group activity potential, especially if you like socializing and throwing parties.

TIP

Electronic items can break down on a regular basis, so it is a good idea to bone up on Mechanical Skills. Until you have a qualified fix-it Sim in the house, you'll be shelling out §50 an hour for a repairman.

FireBrand Smoke Detector

Cost: §50

Motive: None

Notes: Each detector covers one room. At the very least, place a detector in any room that has a stove or fireplace.

SimSafety IV Burglar Alarm

Cost: §250

Motive: None

Notes: An alarm unit covers one room, but an outside alarm covers an area within five tiles of the house. The police are called immediately when the alarm goes off.

SCTC BR-8 Standard Telephone

Cost: §50

Motive: None

Notes: This phone needs a surface, so it's less accessible. Best location is in the kitchen; stick with wall phones in the rest of the house.

SCTC Cordless Wall Phone

Cost: §75

Motive: None

Notes: Place these phones wherever your Sims spend a lot of time.

Urchineer Train Set by Rip Co.

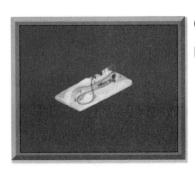

Cost: §80

Motive: Fun (2)

Notes: Group activity; can only be used by kids.

Televisions

Buying a TV is the easiest way to put a little fun into your Sims' lives, and it is a group activity. You can maximize the effect by matching the program category with your Sim's personality, as noted in the following table.

PERSONALITY	FAVORITE TV SHOW
Active	Action
Grouchy (low nice)	Horror
Outgoing	Romance
Playful	Cartoon

Your TV will eventually break down, especially if you have a family of couch potatoes. Do not attempt to repair the TV unless your Sim has at least one Mechanical Skill point (three is even better). If your Sim doesn't have the proper training, poking around inside the TV will result in electrocution.

Monochrome TV

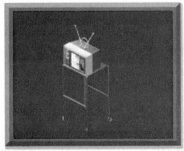

Cost: §85

Motive: Fun (2)

Notes: Strictly for tight budgets, but it gives your Sims a little mindless fun.

Trottco 27" Color Television B94U

Cost: §500

Motive: Fun (4)

Notes: A lazy Sim's favorite activity is watching TV.

Soma Plasma TV

Cost: §3,500

Motive: Fun (6), Room (2)

Notes: It's expensive, but it provides instant entertainment for a full house.

Stereos

Dancing to the music is a great group activity, especially for Sims with effervescent personalities (although it is perfectly acceptable to dance alone). When a Sim dances with a houseguest, it increases both their Fun and Social ratings. You can personalize *The Sims* by placing your own MP3 files in the Music/Stations directory.

"Down Wit Dat" Boom Box

Cost: §100

Motive: Fun (2)

Notes: An inexpensive way to start a party in your front yard.

Zimantz Component Hi-Fi Stereo

Cost: §650

Motive: Fun (3)

Notes: Perfect for your big party room.

Strings Theory Stereo

Cost: §2,550

Motives: Fun (5), Room (3)

Notes: The ultimate party machine, this is the only stereo that enhances your Room score.

Computers

A computer is a Sim's best tool for finding a job. The computer has three job postings every day, making it three times as productive as the newspaper employment ads. Aside from career search, the computer provides entertainment for the entire family, and it helps the kids keep their grades up (better chance of cash rewards from the grandparents). Playful and lazy Sims love the computer. However, if only serious Sims occupy your house, you can grab a newspaper and let the age of technology pass you by.

Moneywell Computer

Cost: §999

Motive: Fun (3), Study

Notes: All you need is a basic computer for job searching.

Microscotch Covetta Q628-1500JA

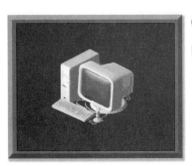

Cost: §1,800

Motive: Fun (5), Study

Notes: More power translates into better gaming.

The Brahma 2000

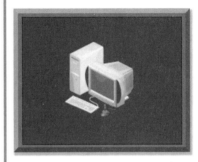

Cost: §2,800

Motive: Fun (7), Study

Notes: More than twice the fun of a basic computer.

Meet Marco

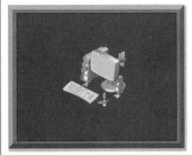

Cost: §6,500

Motive: Fun (9), Study

Notes: For Sim power users—the family will fight for playing time on this beast.

Games

OCD Systems SimRailRoad Town

Cost: §955

Motive: Fun (4), Room (3)

Notes: You need a large area for this train table, but it is an excellent group activity and it gives a serious boost to your Room score.

"See Me, Feel Me" Pinball Machine

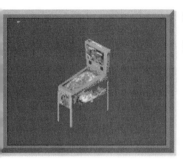

Cost: §1,800

Motive: Fun (5)

Notes: Build a big family room and add a pinball machine to keep your guests occupied for hours.

SRI Virtual Reality Set

Cost: §2,300

Motive: Fun (7)

Notes: Playful Sims have been known to don VR glasses on their way to the bathroom (even with full bladders). For grins, wait until a Sim puts on the glasses, then immediately issue another command. The Sim head on the control panel will wear the glasses for the duration of your game.

Appliances

With the exception of the dishwasher and trash compactor, the Sim appliances are all devoted to the creation of food or java. At a bare minimum, you need refrigeration. However, if you want your Sims to eat like royalty, train at least one family member in the gentle art of cooking and provide that Sim with the latest in culinary tools.

Mr. Regular-Joe Coffee

Cost: §85

Motive: Bladder (-1), Energy (1)

Notes: Only adults can partake of the coffee rush. The effects are temporary, but sometimes it's the only way to get rolling.

Gagmia Simore Espresso Machine

Cost: §450

Motive: Bladder (-2), Energy (2), Fun (1)

Notes: If you want a morning jolt, espresso is the way to go. You'll fill your bladder twice as fast as with regular coffee, but it is a small price to pay for more energy and a splash of fun.

Brand Name Toaster Oven

Cost: §100

Motive: Hunger (1)

Notes: This little roaster is better at starting fires than cooking food. Improve your Cooking Skills and buy a real oven. Until then, use a microwave.

Positive Potential Microwave

Cost: §250

Motive: Hunger (2)

Notes: You can warm up your food without burning the house down.

Dialectric Free Standing Range

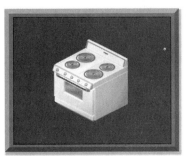

Cost: §400

Motive: Hunger (5)

Notes: After raising your Cooking Skills to three or above, you can create nutritious (and satisfying) meals on this stove.

The "Pyrotorre" Gas Range

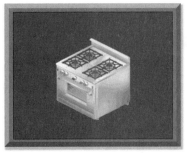

Cost: §1,000

Motive: Hunger (7)

Notes: A skilled chef can create works of art on this stove.

NOTE

Although an expensive stove enhances your Sim meals, it is only one of three steps in the cooking process. To maximize the potential of your stove, you need an excellent refrigerator for storage, and a food processor for efficient preparation.

Wild Bill THX-451 Barbecue

Cost: §350

Motive: Hunger (4)

Notes: Only experienced adult chefs should fire up the barbecue. Be careful not to position the grill near flammable items.

KLR8R Food Processor

Cost: §220

Motive: Hunger (2)

Notes: A food processor speeds up meal preparation and enhances food quality.

Junk Genie Trash Compactor

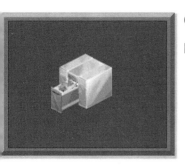

Cost: §375

Motive: None

Notes: A compactor holds more garbage than a trash can, and even when it is full, it will not degrade the Room rating because the trash is concealed.

Dish Duster Deluxe

Cost: §550

Motive: Dirty dishes lower your Room score.

Notes: Kids can't use the dishwasher, but it still cuts cleanup time considerably, and the countertop can be used for placing other items (sorry, no eating allowed).

Fuzzy Logic Dishwasher

Cost: §950

Motive: Dirty dishes lower your Room score.

Notes: The Cadillac of dishwashers cleans up kitchen messes in a snap. This model has fewer breakdowns than the Dish Duster.

Llamark Refrigerator

Cost: §600

Motive: Hunger (6)

Notes: This model is sufficient while your Sims are building up their Cooking Skills.

Porcina Refrigerator Model P1g-S

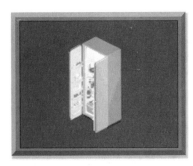

Cost: §1,200

Motive: Hunger (7)

Notes: This model produces more satisfying food for your Sims.

Freeze Secret Refrigerator

Cost: §2,500

Motive: Hunger (8)

Notes: The best place to store your food. When it's matched with a food processor, gas stove, and an experienced chef, your Sims will be licking their lips.

Plumbing

Sims can't carry buckets to the well for their weekly bath, and the outhouse hasn't worked in years, so install various plumbing objects to maintain a clean, healthy environment. Of course, not every plumbing object is essential, but you can't beat a relaxing hour in the hot tub with a few of your closest friends (or casual acquaintances).

Hydronomic Kitchen Sink

Cost: §250

Motive: Hygiene (2)

Notes: Without it the Sims would be washing dishes in the bathroom.

Epikouros Kitchen Sink

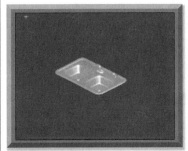

Cost: §500

Motive: Hygiene (3)

Notes: It's twice as big as the single, but a dishwasher is a better investment.

"Andersonville" Pedestal Sink

Cost: §400

Motive: Hygiene (2)

Notes: Neat Sims like to wash their hands after using the toilet.

Hygeia-O-Matic Toilet

Cost: §300

Motive: Bladder (8)

Notes: Hey, your only other option is the floor.

Flush Force 5 XLT

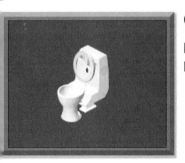

Cost: §1,200

Motives: Comfort (4),
Bladder (8)

Notes: Your Sims can't go to the ballpark to get a good seat, but they can sit in a lap of luxury in the bathroom.

SpaceMiser Shower

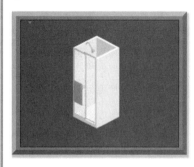

Cost: §650

Motive: Hygiene (6)

Notes: This is basic equipment in a Sims bathroom. One Sim can shower at a time, and the neat ones tend to linger longer than the sloppy ones. Sims are generally shy if they are not in love with a housemate, so you may need more than one shower (and bathroom) to prevent a traffic jam in the bathroom.

Justa Bathtub

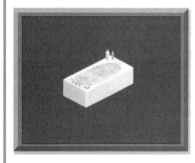

Cost: §800

Motives: Comfort (3),
Hygiene (6)

Notes: Your Sims get a double benefit from a relaxing bath when they have a little extra time.

Sani-Queen Bathtub

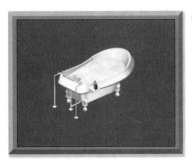

Cost: §1,500

Motives: Comfort (5), Hygiene (8)

Notes: Almost twice the price, but the added Comfort and Hygiene points are worth it.

Hydrothera Bathtub

Cost: §3,200

Motives: Comfort (8), Hygiene (10)

Notes: The most fun a Sim can have alone. Save your Simoleans, buy it, and listen to sounds of relaxation.

WhirlWizard Hot Tub

Cost: §6,500

Motives: Comfort (6), Hygiene (2), Fun (2)

Notes: Up to four adult Sims can relax, mingle, and begin lasting relationships in the hot tub.

Lighting

Sims love natural light, so make sure the sun shines through your windows from every direction. And, when the sun goes down, your Sims need plenty of lighting on the walls, floors, and tables to illuminate their world until bedtime. Although only three lamps listed below have direct impact on the Room score, all of the lamps have a collective effect when spread evenly throughout the home. Pay special attention to key activity areas in the kitchen, family room, bedrooms, and of course, the bathroom.

CAUTION

Lamp bulbs burn out with use, and they must be replaced. Sims can replace their own bulbs, but without Mechanical Skills, they run the risk of electrocution. Hiring a repairman is another option, but at §50 per hour, this can be very costly.

Table Lamps

Bottle Lamp

Cost: §25

Motive: None

ove n' Haight Lava Lamp

Cost: §80

Motive: Room (2)

SC Electric Co. Antique Lamp

Cost: §300

Motive: Room (1)

Ceramiche Table Lamp

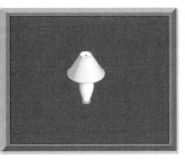

Cost: §85

Motive: None

Floor Lamps

Halogen Heaven Lamp by Contempto

Cost: §50

Motive: None

Elite Reflections Chrome Lamp

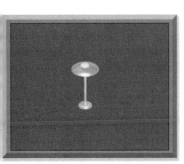

Cost: §180

Motive: None

Lumpen Lumeniat Floor Lamp

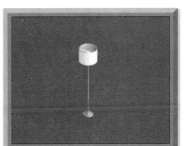

Cost: §100

Motive: None

Torchosteronne Floor Lamp

Cost: §350

Motive: Room (1)

Wall Lamps

White Globe Sconce

Cost: §35

Motive: None

Oval Glass Sconce

Cost: §85

Motive: None

Top Brass Sconce

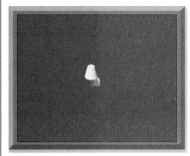

Cost: §110

Motive: None

Blue Plate Special Sconce

Cost: §135

Motive: None

Outside Lamp

Garden Lamp (Outdoor Use Only)

Cost: §50

Motive: None

Miscellaneous

We're down to the objects that are hard to fit into a category—everything from bookcases to beverage bars. Don't make the mistake of ignoring these items because you think they're luxuries; your Sim's life would be extremely difficult without a trash can, alarm clock, and bookcase. Plus, if you want to improve your Sim's Charisma and Body ratings, you'll need a mirror and exercise machine. So, once you install the basic objects in your house, look to the Miscellaneous category for objects that take your Sim's lifestyle to the next level.

SnoozMore Alarm Clock

Cost: §30

Motive: None

Notes: After you set the clock, it will ring two hours before the carpool arrives for every working Sim in your house.

Trash Can

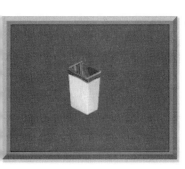

Cost: §30

Motive: None

Notes: Without a place to put trash, your Sim house will become a fly-infested hovel.

Magical Mystery Toy Box

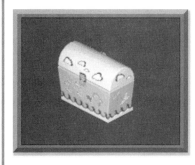

Cost: §50

Motive: Fun (2)

Notes: A good entertainment alternative if your kids are getting bleary-eyed in front of the computer.

Narcisco Wall Mirror

Cost: §100

Motive: Improves Charisma

Notes: Adults can Practice speech in front of the mirror to improve their Charisma.

Medicine Cabinet

Cost: §125

Motive: Hygiene (1), Improves Charisma

Notes: Your Sims can Practice speech in the bathroom and improve their Hygiene at the same time.

Narcisco Floor Mirror

Cost: §150

Motive: Improves Charisma

Notes: Place this mirror anywhere to practice Charisma without locking other Sims out of the bathroom.

Will Lloyd Wright Doll House

Cost: §180

Motive: Fun (2)

Notes: An engaging group activity for kids and adults.

Cheap Pine Bookcase

Cost: §250

Motive: Fun (1), Improve Cooking, Mechanical, and Study Skills

Notes: Reading books is the best way to prevent premature death from fires or electrocution.

"Dimanche" Folding Easel

Cost: §250

Motive: Fun (2), Improves Creativity

Notes: With practice, a Sim can improve Creativity, and eventually sell a picture for up to §166.

Pinegulcher Dresser

Cost: §250

Motive: None

Notes: A Sim can change into various formal, work, and leisure outfits, and even acquire a new body type.

Kinderstuff Dresser

Cost: §300

Motive: None

Notes: Kids like to dress up too!

Amishim Bookcase

Cost: §500

Motive: Fun (2), Improves Cooking, Mechanical, and Study Skills

Notes: This expensive bookcase awards Skill points at the same rate as the cheaper one.

Chuck Matewell Chess Set

Cost: §500

Motive: Fun (2), Improves Logic

Notes: Serious Sims gain the most Fun points by playing, and any two Sims can improve Logic by playing each other.

Traditional Oak Armoire

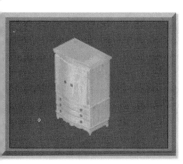

Cost: §550

Motive: Room (1)

Notes: This dresser allows your Sim to change clothes (body skins). The choices vary, depending upon the Sim's current outfit.

SuperDoop Basketball Hoop

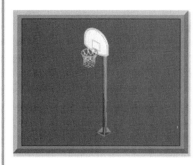

Cost: §650

Motive: Fun (4)

Notes: Active Sims love to play hoops, and any visitor is welcome to join the fun. A Sim with higher Body points performs better on the court.

"Exerto" Benchpress Exercise Machine

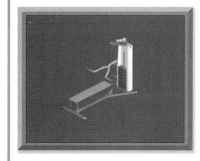

Cost: §700

Motive: Improves Body

Notes: Adult Sims can bulk up their Body points with exercise sessions.

Bachman Wood Beverage Bar

Cost: §800

Motive: Hunger (1), Fun (3), Room (2)

Notes: Every drink lowers the Bladder score, but adult Sims like to make drinks for themselves and friends. Kids can grab a soda from the fridge.

Libri di Regina Bookcase

Cost: §900

Motive: Fun (3), Improves Cooking, Mechanical, and Study Skills

Notes: This stylish bookcase is perfect for a swanky Sim pad, but it still imparts Skill points at the same rate as the pine model.

Antique Armoire

Cost: §1,200

Motive: Room (2)

Notes: A more expensive version of the cheaper armoire, but it adds twice as many Room points.

The Funinator Deluxe

Cost: §1,200

Motive: Fun (5)

Notes: When the house is swarming with kids, send them outside to raise their Fun bar and burn some energy.

Chimeway & Daughters Piano

Cost: §3,500

Motive: Fun (4), Room (3), Improves Creativity

Notes: The most creative Sims will produce more beautiful music. The better the music, the greater the chance that listeners will like it. If a listener does not like the music, both Sims' Relationship scores will deteriorate.

Aristoscratch Pool Table

Cost: §4,200m

Motive: Fun (6)

Notes: Up to two Sims use the table at the same time. Make sure that you allow enough room for Sims to get to the table and walk around it during play.

CHAPTER 7:
ALL IN THE FAMILY

Introduction

Up to this point, we've covered the mechanics of *The Sims*. By now you should be familiar with creating families, building houses, buying objects, and getting jobs; and you should have considerable insight into how a Sim thinks and acts. Now, let's put it all together and join several Sim households in action. In this chapter we introduce you to working Sims families, ranging from one-Sim homes to larger households with kids and babies. Finally, we take an in-depth look at one of the toughest challenges in *The Sims*: building positive (and long-lasting) Relationships.

You Can Make It Alone

The biggest difficulty in being a bachelor is that you have to do everything yourself (sounds like real life, doesn't it?). You'll need to cook, clean, and improve your Skills, while at the same time keep up with a work schedule and satisfy your personal Motives. There's always time for Fun, and a good sofa or easy chair will provide a measure of Comfort. However, it's impossible to socialize while at work, and you will be frustrated watching neighbors drop by during the day and then leave when no one answers the door.

The Single Sim's Career

As a lone Sim you must choose a job that has decent hours and light friendship demands. This leaves a Military career as your only option. At most levels you work a six-hour day, and you won't need a single friend for the first five levels. A promotion to Level 6 requires one friend, but that can be established after you refine your schedule.

Designing a Bachelor Pad

There are several considerations when designing and furnishing a house for one Sim. Review the following checklist before you place your first wall stake.

Fig. 7-1. It's hardly the lap of luxury, but you have everything you need to get a job, keep your sanity, and learn how to cook.

- **Keep your house small, and place the front door close to the street. This allows you to milk a few extra minutes out of every morning before meeting the car pool.**

- **The interior should include a bedroom, bathroom, and living room. Rather than add a family room, use an outside patio area for Fun objects and an exercise machine. A Military career requires an ever-increasing number of Body Skill points.**

- **Install only enough counter space to place a food processor and prepare your meals. This leaves more space for a table and chairs. Buy at least two chairs so that you can socialize with a friend while sharing a meal.**

- **Without the space or the budget to buy expensive sofas or recliners, get a top-of-the-line bed, which enables your Sim to get by on fewer hours of sleep. Buy an inexpensive nightstand for an alarm clock, and add a few wall lights to boost your Room score.**

- **You'll need a computer for your job search, but keep in mind that you can return it within 24 Sim-hours for a full refund. Find your Military job and then pack up the PC.**

Buy an expensive refrigerator to maximize the quality of your food, but don't bother with a stove until your Sim learns how to cook.

Because of your career, there's no need to socialize until you are up for promotion to Level 6, so don't waste money on living room chairs or an expensive sofa. A cheap TV will provide enough Fun for now.

Leaving the Single Life

Eventually you will tire of the solitary lifestyle, which, thanks to the romantic tendencies of most Sims, is not a problem. The first step is friendship. After the Relationship bar tops 70, your Sim needs to lay on the romance, with plenty of kissing and hugging. Eventually, the Propose option will appear on the menu.

Fig. 7-3. "We're alone, the time is perfect, and I've got grass stains on my knee."

Fig. 7-4. "Nope, sorry, I can't marry you on an empty stomach. Besides, your current lover is hiding in the bushes."

Fig. 7-2. The kissin' and huggin' pays off; now it's time to pop the question.

Keep in mind that you have to create potential mates, because the game won't provide them. You might as well choose compatible personalities, and it doesn't hurt to spend some time on career development. Remember that another Sim can also propose to you in his or her house; so unless you want to change residences, hold the romantic interludes at your place.

A marriage proposal can only take place in the home of the proposer, so set the mood (you know, empty your Bladder somewhere other than on the floor, clean up yesterday's dishes, and hide those overdue bills). After accepting the proposal, your new spouse moves into your place, along with a good job (a good thing) and plenty of money (a really good thing). But, proposing does not guarantee a positive response. For example, a Sim will never accept the proposal on an empty stomach, so you might want to eat dinner first.

NOTE

After marriage, your Sim will still share a bed with any other Sim with a high enough Friendship score (over 70), so don't be surprised if your Sim ends up on the couch when his buddy beats him to the sack.

Fig. 7-5. When two Sims decide to get married, they change clothes and complete the ceremony within seconds.

Interestingly, if your future spouse already has children, and at least one adult still resides in his or her original house, the kids stay. So, your new spouse arrives with job and bank account intact, sans kids. What a deal!

That isn't the only unusual aspect of married life in SimsVille. Marriage is not sacred here, at least not in the legal sense. A Sim can have multiple mates all living under the same roof, as pictured in figure 7-6. The interpersonal dynamics can sometimes get a little dicey, but it's workable, and the extra income is great!

Married, with Children

After your Sims promise undying love and devotion to each other (or, at least until the next promotion), it's time to have a baby. Actually, you Sims can live together for years without having children, but if they do, you'll be missing one of the *The Sims'* most vexing experiences.

Conception

The exercise of making a baby is similar to the steps taken to activate the marriage Proposal option. First, get a male and female Sim together, and then concentrate on strengthening their relationship. When both Sims are obviously enjoying each other's company, lay on the hugs and kisses. Keep smooching until you receive the option to have a baby, as pictured in figure 7-7.

Fig. 7-6. After the wedding, our Sim bride goes to bed with her former boyfriend.

Fig. 7-7. A little bundle of joy is jus a click away.

If you answer yes, a bassinet appears almost instantly, amid an explosion of dandelions. The happy couple celebrates the new arrival, then they quickly go back to their daily routine. This baby thing is a snap. Well, not exactly.

Fig. 7-8. Yippee! It's a boy!

In short order, the little bundle of joy starts screaming. A Sim will eventually respond to the cries, but rather than wait, get someone to the baby immediately. Clicking on the bassinet reveals three options: Feed, Play, or Sing. When in doubt, Feed the baby, but be prepared to come right back with Play or Sing when the baby starts wailing again.

Fig. 7-9. Kids do a great job entertaining the baby during one of its frequent crying sessions.

This mayhem continues for three Sim days, during which time the household will be in an uproar. Forget about getting eight hours of beauty sleep. Designate one Sim as primary caregiver, preferably one who does not work, because the baby's cries wake any Sim in the room. The first day is nonstop crying. By the second day, the baby sleeps for a few hours at a time; take advantage of the break and send the caregiver to bed. As long as you stay responsive, the baby evolves into a runny-nosed kid, and the family can get back to normal. However, if you spend too much time in the hot tub and not enough time with the baby, a social service worker will march into your house and take the baby, as pictured in figure 7-10. You'll only receive one warning, so don't take this responsibility lightly.

Fig. 7-10. We hardly knew the little tyke!

NOTE

The bassinet appears near the spot where your Sims made the decision to have a baby. Although the Sims cannot move the bassinet, you can use the Hand Tool to move it. Pick a location that is isolated from other sleeping areas, so the disturbance is kept to a minimum.

Building and Maintaining Healthy Relationships

Gathering an ever-increasing number of friends is critical for career advancement, especially at the higher levels. It is also your Sims' only way to build up their Social scores and fend off frequent bouts of depression. In this section we outline the steps required for finding potential friends, building up positive feelings, and then maintaining healthy relationships.

Talk Is Cheap

The easiest way to make friends is often overlooked, because it is uneventful compared to other social events. However, you can almost always initiate a conversation between Sims (regardless of their Friendship scores), and keep it going for a very long time. During this benign exchange of thought balloons, you can usually nudge the Friendship score in a positive direction. When starting from 0 it takes a few encounters to get over 50 (true friendship), but once you reach this threshold, the action picks up considerably. Our newly married Sims went from a score of 64 to a marriage proposal in one evening. Although the woman eventually declined because her stomach was growling, she proposed the next day and the marriage was consummated.

Fig. 7-11. Keep talking and your Friendship score will grow.

Finding Time to Socialize

After your Sim starts working, it's difficult to find time to call other Sims and arrange meetings. Mornings are worst, although you have more options if your neighborhood has several non-working Sims. Your best bet is to start socializing right after coming home from work. Take care of personal needs first—Hygiene and Bladder—and then "Serve Dinner." Don't let a bad chef get near the stove; you can't afford to waste time putting out a fire or your guests will leave. With a counter full of food, your friends head straight for the kitchen, where you can chat over a plate of Sim-grub and then plan the rest of your evening.

Positive Social Events

After everyone is finished eating, take a little time for pleasant conversation. In the case of the female Sims pictured in figure 7-11, there is a lot of fence mending to accomplish, because one just stole the other's love interest. But, Sims are generally forgiving, and a quarrel can be mended with a few drinks, a game of pool, or a long soak in the hot tub.

Ideally, your house has an entertainment room with group activity items such as a pool table, stereo, or beverage bar. After you get everyone into the room, keep them busy with a string of activities. Even our former lovers can't resist a dance when the music starts playing, as pictured in figure 7-12.

Fig. 7-12. Our Sim guy is enjoying this dance with his former girlfriend, although his current wife will probably slap him when the music stops playing (if she can stay awake long enough).

CAUTION

Avoid close activities such as dancing, hugging, etc. when the current spouse or love interest is in the room. When the dance was over (figure 7-12), our Sim wife did indeed slap her new husband, causing her recently mended Relationship score with the other woman to drop from +14 to –7.

One of the most difficult aspects of entertaining in the evening is keeping the host from falling asleep on the floor. After a hard day's work, most Sims begin nodding out around 10:00 p.m. You can squeeze a little extra time out of the evening if they take a short nap after coming home from work. Be prepared for a grouchy Sim in the morning (figure 7-13) if the evening's festivities stretch too far into the night.

Fig. 7-13. Our tired party girl hurries off to the car pool without a shower—not a good way to impress her superiors.

TIP

After your guests arrive, you need to micromanage your Sims so they don't go off and take care of their own needs. Obviously, you must pay attention to a full Bladder, but you can delay other actions by redirecting your Sims to group activities. Break up the party when your Sims are teetering on the edge of exhaustion or they'll fall asleep on the floor.

CAUTION

Visiting Sims generally hang around until 1:00 a.m. or later, which is undoubtedly past your bedtime. Direct your Sims to bed at the appropriate time, or they may feel compelled to hang out with their guests until well past midnight, as pictured in figure 7-14.

Fig. 7-14. Our host Sim is still cleaning up dishes when he should be asleep.

Stockpiling Potential Friends

When your career advances to the top promotion level, you need more than 10 friends in every career except the Military. Hence, it's a good idea to create a few additional families early in the game, and you might want to fill one house with the maximum of eight Sims to dramatically increase your pool.

Visitors Coming and Going

The following tables include important information on how and why visitors do the things they do. You may not be able to directly control your guests' actions, but at least you won't take it personally when they decide to split.

Visitors' Starting Motives

MOTIVE	STARTING VALUE
Bladder	0 to 30
Comfort	30 to 70
Energy	35
Fun	-20 to 20
Hunger	-30 to -20
Hygiene	90
Social	-50 to -40

In a perfect Sim-world, visitors leave your house just past 1:00 a.m. However if one of their Motives falls into the danger zone, they will depart earlier. When this happens, the Sim's thought balloon reveals a reason for the early exit.

Visitors' Leaving Motives

MOTIVE	DROPS BELOW THIS VALUE
Bladder	-90
Comfort	-70
Energy	-80
Fun	-55
Hunger	-50
Hygiene	-70
Mood	-75
Room	-100
Social	-85

Guest Activities

There are three types of visitor activities: those initiated by a family member, shared activities, and autonomous activities where guests are on their own. The following sections and tables describe each type.

Activities Initiated by Family Member

One of the Sims under your control must prepare food or turn on the TV before visitors can join in. Turning on the TV takes a second, but you need a little prep time for a meal. It's a good idea to begin meal preparation immediately after inviting friends over.

Shared Activities

A Sim can start any of the following activities and then invite the participation of a guest.

OBJECT	VISITORS' INVOLVEMENT
Basketball Hoop	Join
Chess	Join
Dollhouse	Watch
Hot Tub	Join
Pinball Machine	Join
Play Structure	Join
Piano	Watch
Pool Table	Join
Stereo	Join, Dance
Train Set	Watch

Autonomous Activities

Visiting Sims can begin any of the following activities on their own.

Visitors' Autonomous Activities

OBJECT	AUTONOMOUS ACTION
Aquarium	Watch Fish
Baby	Play
Bar	Have a Drink
Chair	Sit
Chair (Recliner)	Sit
Coffee (Espresso Machine)	Drink Espresso
Coffeemaker	Drink Coffee
Fire	Panic
Flamingo	View
Fountain	Play
Lava Lamp	View
Painting	View
Pool	Swim
Pool Diving Board	Dive In
Pool Ladder	Get In/Out
Sculpture	View
Sink	Wash Hands
Sofa	Sit
Toilet	Use, Flush
Tombstone/Urn	Mourn
Toy Box	Play
Trash Can (Inside)	Dispose

Social Interactions

The results of various interactions are best learned by experience because of the individual personality traits that come into play. However, it helps to have an idea what each action may produce. The following table offers notes on each interaction.

INTERACTION	DESCRIPTION
Back Rub	When well-received, it is a good transition into kissing and hugging, but the Relationship score should already be over 50.
Brag	This is what mean Sims do to your Sim. Don't use it, unless you want to ruin a good friendship.
Compliment	Generally positive, but you should withhold compliments until your Relationship score is above 15.
Dance	Great activity between friends (40+), but it almost always causes a jealous reaction from a jilted lover.
Entertain	A somewhat goofy activity, but it usually works well with other Playful Sims.
Fight	Don't do it (unless you know you can take the other Sim!).
Flirt	A great way to boost a strong Relationship (70+) into the serious zone, but watch your back. Flirting usually triggers a jealous reaction from significant others.
Give Gift	A benign way to say you like the other Sim, or that you're sorry for acting like an idiot at the last party; best used with 40+ Relationship scores.
Hug	This one's always fun if the hug-ee's Relationship score is +60; a good transition to kisses, and then a marriage proposal.
Joke	Good between casual friends (+15) who are both Playful.
Kiss	The relationship is heating up, but if a jealous ex or current lover is in the vicinity, someone could get slapped.
Talk	The starting point of every friendship.
Tease	Why bother, unless you don't like the other Sim.
Tickle	Not as positive as it might seem, but Playful Sims are definitely more receptive.

CHAPTER 8:
A DAY IN THE LIFE

Introduction

Now, it's time to turn on our Sim-Cam and follow a few of our families as they handle the ups and downs of Sim life. In this chapter we switch to a scrapbook format, with screenshots of our Sims in interesting—and sometimes compromising—situations. Admittedly, we coaxed our Sims into some of these dilemmas. But it's all in fun, and we think it's the best way for you to get a feel for this amazing game.

As the Sim Turns

Our third adult roommate, Mortimer, just returned home from his night shift, so for now, his needs are secondary. We put him to work mopping the kitchen floor (the dishwasher broke last night, but everyone was falling asleep, so we figured it would keep until morning).

Five o'clock wakeup call is not pretty. Even with full Energy bars, your Sims can be a little cranky, but don't give them any slack. Get the best chef into the kitchen pronto, to serve Breakfast for everyone in the house.

Before we are accused of being sexist, we should explain that the only reason Bella is cooking for everyone is that she is the most experienced chef. If Mark turns on the stove, chances are the kitchen will burn down. We promise to boost his Cooking Skills at the first opportunity.

Switching to Zoomed Out view is a good way to manage the household early in the morning. This way you can quickly target important tasks for completion before the car pool arrives.

Mark is, well, busy at the moment. It's too bad he doesn't gain Energy points for sitting on the toilet, because he stayed up much too late last night. A good breakfast helps, but getting through the day won't be easy, and he can forget about any promotions thanks to his sub-par mood.

It's a nice family breakfast with husband Mortimer on the left, wife Bella on the right, and Bella's ex-boyfriend Mark in the middle. However, there isn't much time for chitchat, because the car pool has arrived, and it will leave at a few minutes past nine.

After canceling his thoughts about sleeping, we click on Mark's car pool. He changes clothes faster than Superman and sprints to his ride in the nick of time. Have a nice day, Mark!

Bella is on her way to the car pool and we have about a half hour to get Mark in gear, which may be a problem due to his low Energy rating. Unfortunately, Bella's Hygiene leaves much to be desired. We make a mental note to get her into the shower before bedtime tonight so she'll be fresh as a daisy in the mornin).

Poor Mortimer! We've been so focused on getting Bella and Mark to work, we didn't notice that the poor slob is asleep on his feet! We need to wake him up (he'll be so happy), and send him to bed.

Uh-oh, big time problem with Mark. He's standing in the kitchen in his pajamas, in a catatonic state. With only a half hour to get to the car pool, we need to shake him up a little and point him to the door.

We receive a reminder that Mortimer's car pool arrives at 4:00 p.m. Unfortunately we forgot to set his alarm, and his Hygiene and Bladder bars have gone south, so we need to wake him up soon. Fortunately, he ate before bedtime, so he can probably get by without a big meal.

Mortimer is up and he's not happy. With the amount of time remaining before his car pool shows up, he can empty his bladder and get in half a shower before racing out the door.

Mark is well rested, so he can fend for himself this morning. He steps into the shower as the car pool arrives, so he has almost one hour to get ready. But, while in the shower, he decides to take the day off and join Bella.

With Mortimer out of the house, we can concentrate on Bella and Mark, who have both arrived home from work. Mark socialized a little too much the night before, so he went straight to bed without any prompting.

The three housemates share a pleasant breakfast together. Perhaps they have finally buried the hatchet after the Mortimer-Bella-Mark thing. We can only hope.

Mortimer arrives home at 1:00 a.m.. After a bathroom break and quick shower, we send him straight to bed so he can party with Bella tomorrow, who has decided to take the day off.

Mark grabs the phone to invite a friend over, but before he can dial, a local radio station calls with great news. He just won §550 in a promotion!

Mark calls a friend, who says he'll be right over. While Mark changes into his Speedo, Mortimer, Jeff, and Bella enjoy a dip in the pool. That's right, Mortimer missed his car pool, too. It's a day off (without pay) for the entire house!

After dinner, Jeff heads for home. Bella and Mark retreat to the den, where Bella rubs Mark's back.

It's on to the hot tub for a long, relaxing soak. Comfort, Hygiene, Social, and Fun scores are soaring. It's too bad we have to eat and empty our Bladders or we'd never leave!

One good rub deserves a hug, as things suddenly heat up between the former lovers.

Everyone will be hungry after the swim and soak, so Bella hops out to make dinner. Soon, everyone grabs a plate and starts discussing what life will be like when they are all unemployed. Everyone, that is, except Mortimer, who prefers standing.

Mortimer takes one look at the lip-locked Sims and heads straight for the bar.

After a couple of adult beverages, Mortimer follows the lovers into the hallway where they are still groping each other like teenagers on prom night.

Bella drives off to work while our two Sim-Neanderthals take their fight to the bathroom.

Mortimer shows his frustration by slapping Mark across the cheek (he's such an animal). Bella is disgusted and goes upstairs to bed.

What will become of our star-crossed lovers?

Will Bella leave Mortimer and go back to Mark?

Will Mark feel guilty about wrecking Mortimer's marriage, and move in with the Newbies?

Will Bella reveal what she and Jeff were really doing in the hot tub?

Who will clean up the bathroom?

For the answers to these burning questions, stay tuned for the next episode of...*As the Sim Turns.*

Life with the Pleasants

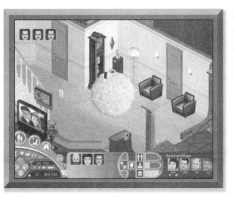

One slap turns to another and seven hours later, Mortimer and Mark are still duking it out.

Jeff experiences the joys of working a night shift—cleaning up his family's dinner dishes...

...and taking out the trash at four in the morning.

Skeeter misses one too many days of school and gets the bad news—he's on his way to military school, never to be seen again.

Everyone is asleep, so Jeff takes an opportunity to practice his Charisma in front of the bathroom mirror. Unfortunately for Jeff, the walking dead also take this opportunity to float through the mirror and scare the •&$%$# out of him.

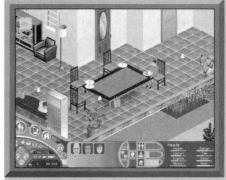

Although his icon has already disappeared from the control panel, Skeeter enjoys one last breakfast before he is exiled from the game.

Like all kids, Daniel and Skeeter can only make snacks on their own, so someone must serve their breakfast before school.

Not wanting to follow in his brother's footsteps, Daniel hits the books and improves his grades.

Hmmm. Which pile should I pay first, the red one or the yellow one? Get a clue, Jeff—if you don't pay the red ones, they'll repossess your furniture!

Pity the Poor Bachelor

With garbage a foot thick on the floor of his house, our bachelor decides to stay outside and entertain a new lady friend with his juggling act.

The Maid should get riot pay for all the garbage this family leaves on the floor!

"Wow, she really likes me! Maybe she won't notice the garbage if I invite her inside."

Maids are limited to cleaning up Sim-messes, but that frees up the family to take care of other important needs, like advancing their skills. Diane Pleasant takes a break to bone up on her Mechanical Skills. Perhaps she can fix the dishwasher and save §50-an-hour repair bills.

"I really like you Bella, so I got you a pair of basketball shoes!"

Bachelors on a fixed budget can have a difficult time having fun. A basketball hoop in the back yard is a good investment, and if you can find a Playful friend, it's a cheap date, too.

"Excuse me, son, could you please move out of the fire so I can extinguish it?"

Kids Are People, Too

Armed with a new gas stove and absolutely no cooking ability, this bachelor decides to flame-broil the kitchen.

Toy boxes are small and relatively inexpensive. If they are placed in the bedroom, your kids can sneak in a little Fun time before school.

Whew, the fireman is here to put out the fire. There's only one problem: he can't get into the house because our hero is standing in front of the stove, which happens to be next to the door. We understand that the bachelor's quarters are tight, but it's probably not a good idea to put the stove next to the front door. By the time the fireman makes his way to the back door, your bachelor could be toast.

Children have fewer inhibitions, but they still don't like to use the bathroom in front of the Maid or their siblings.

Skeeter and Matthew enjoy a little Social and Fun time playing with their railroad town.

Left to their own devices, kids often stay up long past the time their parents hit the sack. In fact, even with Free Will activated, parents feel no responsibility for getting their children to bed early. So, if you forget to send the kids to bed, get ready for some serious tantrums in the morning.

Unlike the railroad, the pinball machine is a solo activity.

Skillful Sims

An exercise machine is the obvious choice for improving a Sim's Body Skill, but if you can keep your Sims in the pool, they'll increase Body scores even faster, and boost Fun at the same time.

Unlike adults, who need toys for their playtime, kids can play with each other.

Sometimes it can be hard to get your Sims to slow down long enough for serious Skill enhancement, especially if it means sitting down to read. The solution is simple: Place two comfortable chairs close to the bookcase, and give each Sim different Skill assignments. Remember that you only need one Cooking expert and one Mechanical expert in the same house. Divide reading assignments appropriately to bring their Skills quickly up to speed.

You might be concerned about an adult male who stands for hours in front of a full-length mirror in his Speedo. However, it makes sense to place a mirror in the family room for easier access. This way, your Sims won't tie up the bathroom practicing Charisma in the mirror over the sink.

Increasing the Creativity Skill through painting has an added bonus—the ability to sell your painting. But, don't get too excited; a bad painting fetches only §1 on the open market.

With minimal Mechanical Skill, repairing this shower seems to take forever, and all the while, Mark's Comfort and Energy scores are dropping. Maybe a Repairman is worth the price until Mark earns a few more Mechanical points.

As the Sim Turns: Part Two

As we return to our Sim soap, Mortimer has just returned from another night shift, and after a light snack, he decides to take an early morning swim, thinking that Mark and Bella are busy getting ready for work. After swimming a few laps, he is ready to go to bed, but wait…where is the ladder?

"I can't get out of the pool!" says Mortimer, frantically. "I'll just tread water for a while until Mark or Bella come out. If I can just…keep… going…getting tired…so tired…."

Mark and Bella finally come outside, but it's too late. Poor Mortimer, exhausted and confused, has already dropped like a stone to the bottom of the pool.

After Mortimer's body is removed from the pool, a tombstone is erected on the spot where the ladder used to be. If Mortimer were still here, he would have appreciated the humor…maybe not.

After getting over the initial shock, Mark and Bella grieve at the site where their "friend" died.

"O.K., enough grieving," says Bella, as she tells Mark a real knee-slapper.

After some welcome comic relief, the two mourners console each other with a supportive hug. Right.

Then, they console each other further...with a dance?

Thinking the time is right (and that they have carried on the charade long enough), Mark pulls Bella close for a kiss. But, much to Mark's surprise, Bella suddenly cools and pushes him away.

What is this strange turn of events?

Did Bella entice Mark into helping her solve the "Mortimer" problem, only to leave him in the lurch?

Find the answers on the next episode of *As the Sim Turns*, **on a computer near you!**

Sims in the Kitchen

In the Motives chapter, we provided a basic explanation of how Sims satisfy their Hunger score. As you know by now, food is readily available in the refrigerator, 24 hours a Sim-day. The supply is endless, and you never have to go to the market. However, the difference between what is in the refrigerator and what a Sim actually eats lies in the preparation. The following screens take you through the various options available to a Sim chef, and the table at the end of this chapter explains how the different appliances and countertops modify the quality of each meal.

After processing the food, Bella throws it in a pot and works her magic. Two more modifiers are at work here: Bella's Cooking Skill and the special features of the Pyrotorre Gas Range.

The snack, a §5 bag of chips, is the lowest item on the Sim food chain. It's better than nothing when your Sim is racing around getting ready for the car pool, but it barely nudges the Hunger bar.

When the meal is finished, Bella places a stack of plates on the counter.

For a much more satisfying meal, direct the best chef in the house to Prepare a Meal. In this screen, Bella is getting ready to throw the raw ingredients into the food processor (a positive modifier, as noted in the table below). While one Sim prepares breakfast, you can assign the other Sims to menial labor, such as mopping or picking up garbage.

Thrilled that he doesn't have to eat his own tasteless slop, Mark grabs a plate from the counter.

Another option for preparing multiple portions is to call out for a pizza. This is a good choice for a Sim who has a low Cooking Skill. Rather than using the stove and setting the kitchen on fire, a telephone call and §40 will buy a hot pie, delivered to the door in an hour.

The Sims love their pizza, and they can't wait to set it down and grab a slice. So, don't be surprised if your Sim plops the carton down on the first available counter—even in the bathroom—and starts grazing.

How Appliances and Surfaces Affect Hunger Score

APPLIANCE/SURFACE	HUNGER POINTS ADDED TO MEAL
Dishwasher	5
Trash Compactor	5
Fridge (Llamark)	9
Toaster Oven	9 (plus Cooking Skill)
Fridge (Porcina)	12
Counter (Barcelona)	16
Counter (NuMica)	16
Counter (Tiled)	16
Fridge (Freeze Secret)	16
Microwave	16 (plus Cooking Skill)
Food Processor	32
Stove (Dialectric)	32 (plus 1.5 x Cooking Skill)
Stove (Pyrotorre)	48 (plus 1.5 x Cooking Skill)

CHAPTER 9:
SURVIVAL TIPS

Introduction

The beauty of playing *The Sims* is that everyone's experience is different. When you take a serious approach to shaping your family, the game can mirror your own life. However, if you mismanage your Sims, they can sink into despair, waving their little arms in the air over failed relationships, poor career decisions, or even a bad mattress. You can always delete your family and start over. But then you would never get that warm, fuzzy feeling that comes from turning your pitiful Sims' world into Shangri La.

This chapter is devoted to the *Sims* player who wants to go the distance and fight the good fight. Because most Sim problems can be traced back to one or more deficient Motive scores, we have arranged the following tips into separate Motive sections. Although some of the information is covered in other chapters, this is meant to be a quick-reference guide for times of crisis. Simply turn to the appropriate Motive and save your Sim's life with one of our game-tested tips.

Of course, you can also take a more devious approach to satisfying or altering your Sim's needs. Our Cheats section gives you a bundle of unofficial commands to rock your Sim's world. We take no responsibility for the results. (In other words, don't come crying to us if you stick your Sim in a room with no doors and he or she drops dead!).

Hunger

Maximize Food Quality and Preparation Time

For the best food quality, upgrade *all* appliances and countertops. Anything short of the most expensive refrigerator, countertop, stove, etc., reduces the potential Hunger value of your meals. Preparing a meal quickly is all about kitchen design. Align your objects in the order of preparation, beginning with the refrigerator, followed by the food processor (figure 9-1), and then ending with the stove (figure 9-2).

Fig. 9-1. The food goes from the refrigerator directly to the food processor.

Fig. 9-2. Next stop is the stove, right next door.

Have an open countertop next to the stove on the other side so the food preparer can set the plates down (figure 9-3). Although it has nothing to do with preparation, position the kitchen table and chairs close to the stove so that your Sims can grab their food, sit down together, and boost their Social scores (figure 9-4).

Fig. 9-5. After making dinner, our hard-working Sim can go to bed and sleep late in the morning.

Fig. 9-3. From the stove, the chef moves just a couple steps to the counter and sets down the plates.

After the food is on the counter, immediately send the Sim to bed. Most Sims should get up by 5, or the very latest, 6 a.m. to be on time for their morning jobs (the chef can sleep in). When everyone comes downstairs, breakfast (it's really dinner, but Sims don't care what you call it, as long as it doesn't have flies) will be on the counter (figure 9-6), fresh and ready to go. You'll save at least 20 Sim-minutes of morning prep time.

Fig. 9-4. If your Sims are prompted to eat, they'll be ready to grab a plate as soon as it hits the counter, and with the table nearby, they can eat, chat, and make it to work on time.

Designate one Sim as your chef. Make sure that Sim has easy access to a chair and bookcase, and then set aside time each day to Study Cooking. When the resident chef's Cooking Skill reaches 10, you have achieved the pinnacle of food preparation.

Make Breakfast the Night Before

Sim food lasts for at least seven hours before the flies arrive and the food is officially inedible. If you have one Sim in the house who doesn't work, have him or her prepare breakfast for everyone at around midnight, as pictured in figure 9-5.

Fig. 9-6. It's only 5:30 a.m., but our Sim kid is already eating breakfast. After taking care of his Hygiene, he'll still have time for studying or boosting his Fun score before the school bus arrives.

Comfort

When You Gotta Go, Go in Style

A toilet is often overlooked as a source of Comfort. The basic Hygeia-O-Matic Toilet costs only §300, but it provides zero Comfort. Spend the extra §900 and buy the Flush Force 5 XLT (figure 9-7). Your Sims have to use the bathroom anyway, so they might as well enjoy the +4 Comfort rating every time they take a seat.

Fig. 9-8. Our Sim is hungry, but he always has time to receive a nice Back Rub.

Fig. 9-7. You can live with a black-and-white TV for a while, but it doesn't make sense to do without the added comfort of the Flush Force.

Hygiene

Your Mother Was Right

One of the biggest contributors to declining Hygiene is the lack of hand washing after using the bathroom (in the Sims and in real life). If your Sim does not have a Neat personality, you may need to initiate this action. If you keep it up throughout the day, your Sim will be in better shape in the morning, when a shorter shower can be the difference between making the car pool or missing a day of work.

Rub Your Sim the Right Way

Giving another Sim a Back Rub is a great way to increase your chances of seeing Hug, and eventually Kiss on the social interaction menu. However, don't forget that it also raises the recipient's Comfort level. If your Sim's Comfort level is down, even after a long night's sleep, try a few Back Rubs. It will send your Sim to work in a better mood, which might be just enough to earn the next promotion.

Fig. 9-9. This Sim has an average Neat rating, which means she won't always wash her hands after using the bathroom. A few gentle reminders are in order.

Flush Your Troubles Away

Sad but true, sloppy Sims don't flush (figure 9-10). It's easy to overlook this nasty habit during a busy day, but it could lead to trouble. A clogged toilet may not affect Hygiene directly, but if your Sim is forced to pee on the floor because the toilet is not working, the Hygiene score drops dramatically.

Fig. 9-10. Second time tonight for this soldier, and we're still waiting for the first flush.

Bladder

Sorry, there's no magic formula for relieving a full Bladder. However, to guard against emergencies and the resulting puddles on the floor, try building two semi-private stalls in your bathroom. This allows two Sims to use the facilities without infringing on each other's privacy, as pictured in figure 9-11.

Fig. 9-11. Dual stalls improve the traffic flow (and other flows) in the bathroom.

Energy

Getting Enough Sleep with Baby

Nothing drains a Sim's Energy bar faster than having a baby in the house (figure 9-12). If you want to survive the three-day baby period without everyone losing their jobs, you must sleep when the baby sleeps. Most likely, this will be in the middle of the day, because Sim babies, like their real counterparts, couldn't care less about their parents' sleep schedules. The baby will not sleep for a full eight hours; however, if you get five or six hours of sleep with the baby, you'll have enough Energy to carry out other important household tasks.

Fig. 9-12. This Sim mom is at the end of her rope, and the baby is just getting warmed up.

Kids Make Great Babysitters

It does nothing for their Fun or Social levels, but Sim kids will dutifully care for their baby siblings. When they come home from school, feed them, allow a short play period, and then lock them in the room with the baby (if you're feeling particularly sadistic, you can go into Build mode and wall them in). They usually respond on their own, but you can always direct them to the crib, as pictured in figure 9-13, (unless they are too exhausted and need sleep). Take advantage of this time by sending the regular caregiver to bed for some much-needed sleep.

Fig. 9-13. Big brother makes a great nanny.

Favorite Fun Activities

TRAIT	BEST ACTIVITIES
Neat	N/A
Outgoing	TV (Romance), Hot Tub, Pool (if Playful is also high)
Active	Basketball, Stereo (dance), Pool, TV (Action)
Lazy	TV (as long as it's on, they're happy!), Computer, Book
Playful	Any fun object, including Computer, Dollhouse, Train Set, VR Glasses, Pinball, etc. If also Active, shift to Basketball, Dance, and Pool.
Serious	Chess, Newspaper, Book, Paintings (just let them stare)
Nice	Usually up for anything
Mean	TV (Horror)

Fun

Finding the Right Activity for Your Sim

Unless your Sims live in a monastery, you should have plenty of Fun objects in your house. The trick is matching the right kind of activity with a Sim's personality. In the frenzy of daily schedules and maintaining Relationships, it's easy to lose touch with your Sim's personality traits. Visit the Personality menu often (click on the "head" icon) to review the five traits. Make sure you have at least one of the following objects readily available to your Sim (the bedroom is a good spot).

When in Doubt, Entertain Someone

If your Sim does not have access to a Fun activity, simply Entertain someone for an instant Fun (and Social) boost, as pictured in figure 9-14. You can usually repeat this activity several times, and it doesn't take much time (great for kids on busy school mornings).

NOTE

A Sim should have at least six points (bars) in one of the following traits to maximize the recommended activity. Of course, an even higher number produces faster Fun rewards. To qualify for the opposite trait (e.g., Active/Lazy, Playful/Serious) a Sim should have no more than three points in the trait).

Fig. 9-14. When a good toy is not around, Sim kids love to Entertain each other.

Social

Satisfying Social requirements can be very frustrating, especially when Sims are on different work or sleep schedules. Socializing is a group effort, so plan small parties on a regular basis. Keep a notepad with all of your Sims' work schedules, so you know whom to invite at any time of the day.

- **It's O.K. to ask your guests to leave. After you shmooze a little and boost your Relationship score, send the Sim packing, and call up a different one. Use this round-robin approach to maintain all of your friendships.**

- **Don't let Mean Sims abuse you. This can be tough to control if you're not paying attention. When you're socializing with a Mean Sim, keep an eye on the activity queue in the screen's upper-left corner. If that Sim's head pops up (without you initiating it), it probably says "Be Teased by...," or "Be Insulted by...." Simply click on the icon to cancel the negative event and maintain your Relationship score. Once you diffuse the threat, engage the Sim in simple talking, or move your Sim into a group activity (pool table, hot tub, pool, etc.)**

- **Unless you like being the bad guy, don't advertise your advances toward one Sim if you already have a Relationship with another. Sims are extremely jealous, but you can still maintain multiple love relationships as long as you don't flaunt them in public.**

Room

A Room score crisis is easy to remedy. If you have the money, simply add more lights and paintings. Also check the quality of objects in the room, and upgrade whenever possible. If your room is jammed with expensive objects, lights, and paintings and your Room score is still low, there must be a mess somewhere. A normally maxed out Room score can slip with so much as a puddle on the floor (as pictured in figure 9-15). Clean up the mess to restore the Room score to its normal level.

Fig. 9-15. It looks like someone fell short of the toilet. A mop will take care of the mess and raise the Room score.

Scan your house on a regular basis for the following negative Room factors:

- **Dead plants**
- **Cheap objects (especially furniture)**
- **Puddles (they can also indicate a bad appliance; when in doubt, click on the item to see if Repair comes up as an option)**
- **Dark areas**
- **If you have the money, replace items taken by the Repo guy.**

Cheats

Activate the cheat command line at any time during a game by pressing Ctrl + Shift + C . An input box appears in the screen's upper left corner. Type in one of the codes listed below. You must re-activate the command line after each cheat is entered. The following cheats work only with Version 1.1 or later of *The Sims*.

Cheats

DESCRIPTION	CODE INPUT
1,000 Simoleans	rosebud
Import and load specific FAM file	import <FAM file>
Create moat or streams	water_tool
Create-a-character mode	edit_char
Display personality and interests	interests
Draw all animation disabled	draw_all_frames off
Draw all animation enabled	draw_all_frames on
Execute "file.cht" file as a list of cheats	cht <filename>
Floorable grid disabled	draw_floorable off
Floorable grid enabled	draw_floorable on
Map editor disabled	map_edit off
Map editor enabled	map_edit on
Move any object (on)	move_objects on
Move any object (off)	move_objects off
Preview animations disabled	preview_anims off
Preview animations enabled	preview_anims on
Quit game	quit
Rotate camera	rotation <0-3>
Save currently loaded house	save
Save family history file	history
Selected person's path displayed	draw_routes on

DESCRIPTION	CODE INPUT
Selected person's path hidden	draw_routes off
Set event logging mask	log_mask
Set free thinking level	autonomy <1-100>
Set game speed	sim_speed <-1000-1000>
Set grass change value	edit_grass <number>:
Set grass growth	grow_grass <0-150>
Set maximum milliseconds to allow simulator	sim_limit <milliseconds>
Set sim speed	sim_speed <-1000-1000>
Sets the neighborhood directory to the path	<directory path>
Start sim logging	sim_log begin
End sim logging	sim_log end
Swap the two house files and updates families	swap_houses <house number> <house number>
Ticks disabled	sweep off
Ticks enabled	sweep on
Tile information displayed	tile_info on
Tile information hidden	tile_info off
Toggle camera mode	cam_mode
Toggle music	music
Toggle sound log window	sound_log
Toggle sounds	sound
Toggle web page creation	html
Total reload of people skeletons, animations, suits, and skins	reload_people
Trigger sound event	soundevent

PART II:

The SIMS™
Unleashed
SPIKE
EXPANSION PACK

CHAPTER 10: WHAT'S NEW IN THE NEIGHBORHOOD

Introduction

In this chapter we hop on the Old Town Shuttle and visit each of the seven new Community Lots in *The Sims Unleashed*. We cover the new objects, personalities, and activities your Sims will find in each location. Finding your way around Old Town is easy thanks to the expanded Neighborhood screen. A series of theme icons lets you locate the Community Lots that interest you, as displayed in the following screenshots.

Shopping Locations

Dog and Cat Adoption Centers

Gardening Shops

Small Pet Shops

Food Service Areas

Recreational Areas

NOTE

If you have The Sims Vacation *installed, another icon for Lodging is activated. In the opening Neighborhood screen, you can go straight Downtown if you have* The Sims Hot Date *installed and to Vacation Island if you add* The Sims Vacation.

When a Sim makes arrangements to visit Old Town, the entire family comes along, even the pets. It takes about 20 minutes for the Old Town Shuttle to reach its destination. However, while your Sim is out shopping, your house stays the same, including the time of day you left. Your Sim's Motives are active while in Old Town. So, you may leave your house at noon, spend several hours away, and come home ready for a shower and a good night's sleep, despite the fact it is lunchtime.

TIP

Allow enough time to complete important tasks when you return from a trip to Old Town. Plan the timing of your visits to maintain a schedule that enables your Sim to satisfy critical Motives and still be ready for work the next morning.

Custer's Market

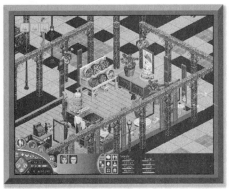

When your Sim's green thumb acts up, the only place to find relief is at Custer's Market, where you can buy seeds or vegetables, ask Gardener Bob for advice, and meet and greet other gardening enthusiasts. There are also seeds and a vegetable stand at the Gothic Quarter. Gardener Bob hangs out there to enjoy the smooth sounds of saxophonist extraordinaire, W. C. Friendly.

No espresso bars or live music at Custer's Market. The best you can hope for is a good song out of Giuseppi Renni and Mr. McCutch.

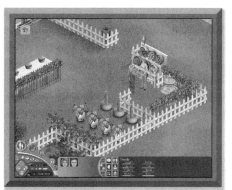

If your garden is bare, you can buy produce at the vegetable stand. After your first harvest, you can return here and sell your veggies (Carrots: §7, Lettuce §6, Tomatoes: §4, and Beans: §4). If your garden produces a super yield, sell it to Gardener Bob, who forks over a cool §150 (for details, read the following section about Gardener Bob's Plant Tonic).

After preparing a Victory Garden patch at your house, buy the seeds of your choice at the large floor display or counter.

Gardener Bob is a wealth of information on storing and selling vegetables, tending your garden, dealing with pests, and buying plant tonic.

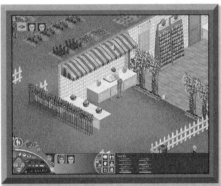

Gardening enthusiasts are an earthy bunch, so don't expect fancy bathrooms for your Sims' Bladder needs. The best you'll get are a couple of Port-A-Potties and an outdoor washbasin.

Tending Your Garden

Buying seeds is the easy part of starting a garden. It's after the seeds go in the ground that the hard work begins. You must water and weed regularly, and as your garden grows, pest control becomes a factor (see the Garden Pests section for valuable tips). Here is a checklist for producing a bountiful harvest and storing your fresh vegetables.

- **Don't plant too many plots; you'll have difficulty keeping up with regular maintenance.**
- **Daily water each active garden plot.**
- **Weed promptly to keep a plot's output at the maximum level.**
- **Tomatoes and Beans continue to grow after each harvest without replanting.**
- **Carrots and Lettuce require replanting after each harvest.**
- **Buy a pantry to store your vegetables.**

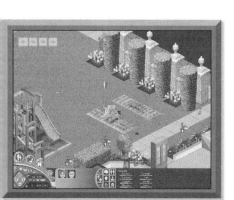

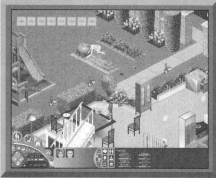

When you start accumulating fresh vegetables, buy a Never Cold Food Hold or Pantry de Provence for storage. You can use either model to store homegrown vegetables or those purchased at the vegetable stand.

Gardener Bob's Plant Tonic

Spending §35 on Gardener Bob's Plant Tonic does not guarantee a successful harvest. The tonic carries a 15 percent chance of destroying your garden plot and a 25 percent chance of producing a super yield. Sell a super yield to Gardener Bob (it won't fit in your pantry) for a whopping §150.

Garden Pests

Bunnies are cute and cuddly, and they improve the Room score of your garden. But, they can make short work of a Carrot plot. Your garden advertises for bunnies after you plant three plots of Carrots. The garden is checked twice a day with a 20 percent likelihood of their arrival. After the cottontails move in, they hang around for three days unless you are heartless enough to order your cat to hunt them. The cats don't mind, because they earn Hunting points, while satisfying Hunger and Fun.

Unlike bunnies, there is nothing cute about gophers. They arrive with regularity after you plant six garden plots of any crop, and they are destructive. Scarecrows, Windmills, and Gnomes ward off gophers by limiting their pillaging to one plot,

then scaring them away for a time. Without these items, the gophers keep digging until your garden is a shambles.

TIP The Gardening Gnome is available with the Living Large expansion pack, and Windmills are available with the Hot Date expansion pack.

A more permanent solution than a Scarecrow is to set your cat on the gophers. Cats love to hunt gophers as much as they love terrorizing bunnies. When the obnoxious critters go down for the count, the gopher holes are gone and your cat earns 15 Hunting Skill points, not to mention a Fur and Hunger boost.

TIP Stray cats will attack gophers on sight, so if you have a sizable garden, don't shoo the freeloading felines away.

McArthur Square

When the same four walls give your Sim the blues, call the Old Town Shuttle and visit McArthur Square. For refreshment, buy a cup of coffee and a pastry, listen to the strolling saxophone player, and enjoy the fountains. You can also view the Birds in the large cage; for more hands-on entertainment, feed a cracker to the cockatoo.

The outdoor café area is a pleasant spot for munching a high-calorie dessert and listening to music. If you can stop eating long enough, make a new friend. View the birdcage for a little Fun, or listen to the strolling saxophone player.

Like other social interactions at MacArthur Square, feeding the cockatoo is not a sure thing. You might lose a finger for your trouble, be screamed at by a nasty Bird, or enjoy a pleasant exchange.

If your Sim is having a tough time making friends, he or she can always stare at the fountain.

With a large playground area, MacArthur Square is a great place to bring the kids.

Lake Barrett

When your Sim's social life is suffering, hop the Old Town Shuttle to Barrett Hall. There your Sim can mingle with other Sims, shoot pool, sip coffee, or listen to music. If you don't like the action downstairs, wander up to the second floor for a more intimate atmosphere. Unlike the family parks, such as McArthur Square or Sim Central, Barrett Hall is frequented by more adult Sims, so your chances for friendship or romance are better. In fact, you might want to sleep all day so you can listen to jazz until the wee hours.

A cup of triple-strength espresso will give your night owl Sim a much needed boost.

A night on the town means a night away from responsibilities. If Fido pees on the floor, someone else will clean it up. It's worth the cost of a drink to experience it.

Unlike the Port-A-Potties at Custer's Market, the bathroom at Lake Barrett is first rate.

The pool hall on the lower level is always busy. Find another Sim for a rousing game of nine-ball to boost your Fun and Social scores.

Pet Paradise

When you are ready to adopt a furry Sim (not to be confused with Elden Hick), visit Pet Paradise to pick out a puppy or kitten. You can also buy object-based pets, including Birds, Fish, Iguanas, and Turtles. Pet Paradise is a full-service store, with merchandise (Pet Treats, Collars, Ribbons, and Toys), and a bathing area for your dog (cats clean themselves).

You'll also find the Pet Trainer in the display pen area. Unpon request, he will dispense free tips on Obedience, Housebreaking, Tricks, Breeding, and Hunting. The Pet Trainer would like you to pay him for his services, which include training your pet to Bounce, Flip Low, Flip High, and Jump. For more information on training your pet and entering it in a Pet Show, see the Dogs and Cats chapter.

Adopting a pet is the featured activity at Pet Paradise. Your Sim can play with the animal first, then select the pet for adoption (you can also pick the breed, so your choice is not limited to the animal originally displayed in the pen).

After adopting a pet, it is added to your family. You can play with it or hire the Pet Trainer. This takes time, so Browse the flea collars and chew toys for a while.

You can also buy object-based pets at the Pet Paradise, including Birds (budgies and lovebirds), Iguanas, Turtles, and Fish. For more information on their care and interactions, see the Birds, Fish, Turtles, and Iguanas chapter.

After adopting a pet, you can buy Toys, treats, and spiked collars. Pet Paradise is happy to take your simoleans for a wide variety of accessories.

Of course, the family dog loves a trip to Pet Paradise. There is plenty of kibble, a place to crash, and even a tub for a quick midnight bath.

There are better places to eat in Old Town than the Pet Paradise, but if your Sim is starving, the outdoor pastry stand provides a quick sugar fix while you're waiting for the trolley.

Old Town Quarter

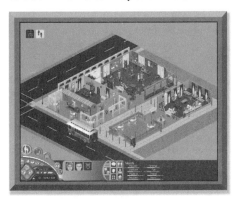

The Old Town Quarter is a perfect destination when you want a little of everything. Where else can you go to eat pastry, listen to jazz, and play computer games all in the same room? If you'd rather shop till you drop, you can browse the masks and candles, or have your palm read (wash your hands first). Wander upstairs, where you'll find a small pet shop in one building and a pool hall in the other.

The small pet shop is a great place to watch the Birds (the cats love it), feed the parrot and cockatoo, or buy lovebirds and budgies.

In the pool hall, you can play chess...

...shoot billiards...

...or have quality time with your pet.

The only bathrooms are located on the second floor, above the gift shop, so don't wait too long to go! With an empty Bladder, you'll have more time to spend shopping downstairs. Buy an exotic wall mask or a creepy candle, or have Ms. Lucille tell you what the future holds.

CAUTION

Unlike at the Pet Paradise, your dog cannot eat at Old Town Quarter, so his mood will gradually deteriorate while your Sim is having a good time. Don't ignore your pet's needs while cruising Old Town, or that sweet little puppy is likely to bite you the next time you settle in for a little snuggling.

Gothic Quarter

The Gothic Quarter is a strange haunt that appeals to the Goths, for obvious reasons. The complex includes a café, complete with vegetable stand and Gardener Bob. Above the café is a small billiard room that includes a cushy bed for your pet. Across from the café, you can stroll through a gloomy cemetery. What better place to meet your future mate? Finally, the retail shop includes candles, masks, Ms. Lucille, and a comfortable library area where your Sim can chill with a good book.

No trip to Gothic Quarter is complete without Ms. Lucille reading your palm. She may even see romance in your future!

If you are short on simoleans, walk by the displays, grab a book, and relax on the comfortable sofa. You might find a friend on the other side of the couch!

Palm Readings for Sims and Pets

Paying §20 for a palm reading doesn't seem like a good investment, but depending on Ms. Lucille's reading, your Sim and/or pet can receive an instant payoff. The following lists include possible readings and their corresponding results.

Your Sim receives nothing, if Ms. Lucille says the following:

- Your back pocket is a little bit lighter now, which probably shows that you will have less back problems in the future. It isn't good to carry a lot of weight around like that. Smart move coming to see me.

- Your career is not going to advance itself, you need to be a bit more active about making friends and influencing people. Once you've impressed all the right people, you're sure to move up.

- Pets can be wonderful friends, but you really need to get out more and meet some people! Do not deny yourself a full plate of life, just because you are a shy individual.

- Energy is spread too thinly across your life. Focus on that which truly matters to you and do not spend your energy carelessly. This can only mean one thing: go out and purchase a hot tub immediately. I fear your very life may depend on it!

Your entire Sim's family receives a maximum boost to all Motives if Ms. Lucille says:

- I see a change in your life. More importantly, marriage in your near future. You are uncertain if this is a good thing, but I assure you it is. Love will again find a place in your heart.

Motives are filled to the maximum for the Sim receiving the palm reading, if Ms. Lucille says the following:

- I can see by your life line, that you are still alive, this is good. Your energy levels are very good, however I caution you around the elements of fire and water. I feel these forces may threaten your very existence, probably not though.

Your pet receives nothing, if Ms. Lucille says:

- This pet will make some friends which will become VERY important to your career growth, but you need to take this pet to the park frequently for this to happen.

- I see a raccoon attacking your trash can at home! It is waking up everyone in the house and making a total mess! But lo...this pet will thwart the raccoon and chase it away!

- I see this pet chasing off one of your neighbors. You will think it is a bad act by your pet, but this neighbor meant you harm. You should praise your pet for this, they are doing you a favor.

- I see this pet making a total mess in your house. They have gotten into the trash, Oh No! They're spreading it all over...this will soon bring a skunk to your house!

Your pet receives -100 Hygiene if Ms. Lucille says:

- I see a skunk in this pet's future. While it means well, it will go and attack the skunk. It's just trying to protect its master, but it gets sprayed! I see you bathing this pet over and over….

Your pet receives a maximum boost to all Motives if Ms. Lucille says:

- I see this pet winning the Blue Ribbon at the pet show! You will breed this pet and start a long line of award winning pets!

Not much to do in the cemetery, but look at Sim graves.

Gothic Quarter features the plushest bathroom accommodations, located above the retail shop.

The small billiards room is pleasant, but it doesn't attract as many players as Lake Barrett.

The little café at Gothic Quarter packs several activities into a small but cozy area. Sip coffee, eat pastry, play chess, or buy vegetables. And, you can do it all while W. C. Friendly works his magic on the saxophone.

Sim Central Park

CHAPTER 10: WHAT'S NEW IN THE NEIGHBORHOOD

The last stop on our tour is Sim Central Park, where your Sim family can frolic in the grass, play basketball, swim, or enter a Pet Show (for details on training for and entering Pet Shows, see the Dogs and Cats chapter). Sim kids love the playground equipment.

Between the maintenance person and guests, the small bathroom facility gets a workout. Maybe it's the close proximity to the pool. All that water is hard on a Sim's Bladder.

The Pet Show is the featured event at Sim Central Park. However, the competition is tough, and your pet must be well-trained if you want to walk away with anything higher than a booby prize (for expert dog training tips, see the Dogs and Cats chapter). But, even if your dog bites the judge, you can drown your sorrows with a chocolate éclair at the pastry counter.

CHAPTER 11: DOGS AND CATS— THE STARS OF THE SHOW

Introduction

At first glance, the addition of pets to *The Sims* seems to be little more than a pleasant distraction from career advancement, food preparation, and bladder control. But, after a few days with a new puppy, you realize that your Sim family will never be the same. A family pet is a perpetual source of entertainment, and after you get past the horrors of housebreaking, you begin to look at your pet as more of a friend and companion rather than an escapee from the pound. In this chapter, we take a close-up look at Dogs and Cats, with tips on care, training, and breeding. After covering the basics, we take our pet on the road, providing a glimpse at how your pet relates to the Sim world outside of your family.

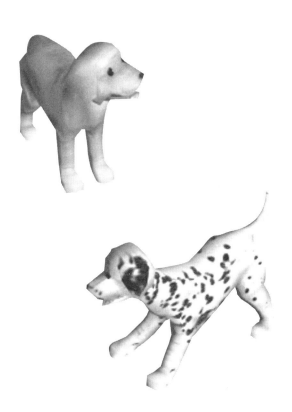

A Trip to Pet Paradise

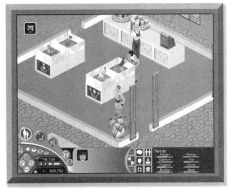

Pet ownership begins with a trip to Pet Paradise, where you can adopt a puppy or kitten for §399. You can choose to adopt a pet, at which point you are presented with the interface to select the pet's breed. If you only wish to browse and not buy, select "Cancel," which cancels the adopt interaction.

After selecting your pet's breed and sex and choosing a name, you pay the cashier and take ownership. The new animal appears alongside you in the store, eager to meet its new owner. After a little bonding, you are on your way. Although the new pet hangs around initially, don't become alarmed when it takes off to explore the area. You are easily reunited with a quick call, and when you board the shuttle for the trip home (or to another Old Town location), your new Dog or Cat will be right behind you.

There is no need to buy accessories after adopting a pet, but you might as well take advantage of Pet Paradise while you're there. Here is a list of available products and their functions.

* **Pet Treats (§45):** excellent reinforcement for obedience and trick training, provides a one-time Hunger boost
* **Squeaky Tara Pet Toy (§25):** play toy for Dogs and Cats
* **Gnawhide Pet Toy (§49):** for Dogs only, provides more Fun than Rubber Duck
* **Marty McMousenip catnip (§)45:** for Cats only, provides more Fun than Rubber Duck
* **Cat and Dog Collars (§15-25):** assorted styles and colors (in separate displays)

There is plenty for your pet to do at Pet Paradise while you shop. Food dishes are full, houses and beds are available for Cat (or Dog) naps, and your pet is free to nuzzle or nip another Sim. Animals with excess energy can even burn off calories on the playground. For a good laugh, don't miss your pet going down the slide.

NOTE

For the most part, pets are self-sufficient at Pet Paradise. Unlike your Sims, they can find a comfortable place to sleep, so there is no need to closely monitor their Motives. Check on them to make sure they aren't biting a friend.

Meet the Pet Trainer

After adopting your pet, you can go home and begin housebreaking (Dogs only) or training. However, if you have the simoleans, you can squeeze in a few sessions with the Pet Trainer before you leave. Or, if you'd rather handle the training yourself, you can receive free advice on Obedience, Housebreaking, Tricks, Breeding, and Hunting (Cats only).

In addition to the cost (first session is §250, and it goes up from there), training is time consuming. Monitor your Sims' Motives to determine how long you can hang around. The Pet Trainer teaches your Dog or Cat how to do Tricks (Housebreaking and Obedience are up to you). As your Dog successfully completes a training session, each successive session becomes more expensive, as illustrated in the following table. It takes 10 training sessions to reach the maximum level of Trick skills.

SESSION #	COST
1	§250
2	§300
3	§350
4	§400
5	§450
6	§500
7	§550
8	§600
9	§650
10	§700

Training Your Pets

The Sims Unleashed pets cannot hold down jobs, so their Skills menu contains three bars: Housebreaking (Dogs only), Hunting (Cats only), Tricks, and Obedience. You can train your pet in these areas, and if you aspire to winning a 1st place ribbon at the next Pet Show, develop Tricks and Obedience skills. The following sections include specific tips and instructions for training Dogs and Cats.

Housebreaking

Dogs

Eventually, you must go home with your new puppy and begin training. The first priority is to get your Dog to stop peeing on the carpet, which it will do almost immediately after walking through the front door. This is a simple but time consuming process of scolding the Dog when you find a puddle. Each time you scold the Dog, it gains a point on the Housebreaking bar. After 10 "incidents," your Dog is officially housebroken, and it will go outside. Fortunately, this is a lifetime skill that does not require reinforcement.

TIP

A Dog considers any area outside the house fair game for emptying its bladder. This includes your nice stone patio, so, if you don't want to deal with unsightly puddles during a garden party, locate your patio away from the rear door of the house. Although you can direct your Dog to go to a certain area, Sim life is too busy to monitor this on a regular basis.

If the idea of scolding your puppy doesn't appeal to you, positive reinforcement is another option. However, be forewarned that this will occupy a good portion of your day as you monitor the Dog's Bladder Motive. A young Dog is very erratic as to picking a time to go. Your only real warning is when the Dog starts to circle around or move back and forth while sniffing the ground. If you direct the Dog outside and witness the act, you can immediately praise the Dog, which has the same effect as a scolding. If you are a master micro-manager, you can even direct the Dog to pee in the garden, which saves you from watering.

You would think that forcing a Dog to do tricks in a puddle would inspire faster housebreaking, but no such luck. However, you should clean up the mess to keep your Room score up.

TIP

A well-placed Fire Hydrant "advertises" to a Dog whose Bladder Motive is at least 50 percent full.

When your Dog is housebroken, it will usually go to the farthest reaches of your property when nature calls. However, even a housebroken Dog leaves an occasional calling card close to the house. If left to accumulate, the little piles can degrade the area's Room score, so it's a good idea to scoop the poop regularly.

Cats

Housebreaking is a nonfactor when it comes to adopting a Cat. Buy a litter box (Dunginator 9000) and place it in an accessible, but not too obvious, position. You never have to worry about a Cat making a mess inside, but you do need to regularly clean the litter box, or your Room score takes a serious hit. Furthermore, a litter box has a capacity of 15 uses before your Cat will refuse to step inside. At this point, the Cat will go on the floor, so it pays to clean the box regularly (another good reason to hire a maid).

Obedience

Dogs

With Housebreaking out of the way, you are left with Tricks and Obedience (Sit and Stay). Unlike Tricks, you cannot hire the Pet Trainer to teach your Dog Obedience, so we recommend getting started here first. Don't expect too much from your first few sessions of Sit and Stay. However, the process is cumulative, so each time you train the pet, the progress bar picks up from the last session. As your pet's Obedience skill improves, the Sit and Stay challenges become increasingly more difficult as your Sim turns her back to the animal or even engages in activities in a different room.

NOTE

When your Dog reaches the top level of Obedience, don't forget to release it from Sit and Stay, or it will stay in position indefinitely!

Cats

The concept of Obedience training is exactly the same for Cats as it is for Dogs. The process is slow but cumulative, and you must keep coming back for repeated sessions until your Cats are in show-shape.

Tricks

Dogs

Teaching your Dog tricks requires patience, especially in the beginning. A pet is just as likely to ignore your Sim's request or even get nasty if the session goes on too long (biting your pants cuff is a good indication of boredom). However, your Dog eventually will perform like a champ. The Tricks menu includes: High Flip, Bounce, Jump, Low Flip, and Play Dead (when your Dog is still mastering a trick, the menu displays Train Bounce, Train High Flip, etc.).

High Flip

Bounce

Jump

Low Flip

Play Dead

CAUTION

Trick Skills deteriorate over time if they are not periodically reinforced.

Cats

Training to be a Cat boxer.

Learning a few Cat show tunes.

Play Keyboard

Ultra-independent Cats do not come to mind as Trick animals, but they have a sense of style that is perfectly featured in *The Sims Unleashed.* No fetching or doing flips for Sim Cats. The trick menu includes Box, Dance, and Play Keyboard, and the performances are memorable. The training process is exactly the same as for Dogs. Hire the Pet Trainer at Pet Paradise for an accelerated course, or take the long route and train your Cat at home.

Box

Dance

Like Dogs, Cats can become impatient or act downright nasty when asked to train or perform. If they are hungry or tired, your chances for a positive session are greatly reduced. Instead of following your Sim's cue, your cute kitty may rear back and hiss, giving you a clear signal that the show will definitely not go on.

Hunting

Cats

Instead of Housebreaking, a Cat's Pet Skills menu includes Hunting. This is an entertaining and useful talent for a busy Sim's household. If you fall behind on your cleaning, garbage piles breed flies, and if you have a Cat in the house, the flies eventually turn into mice. When you see several little white rodents running around in circles, click on your Cat and select Hunt. The number of Eek!Mice! selections on the Hunt menu corresponds to the number of infestations.

After instructing your Cat to Hunt, it will look for the mice, although you can speed up the process by telling your Cat to go to the mice. When the Cat finds its prey, the screen goes mercifully blurry to save you from witnessing the carnage. After a few moments, the mice are gone, except for one lifeless body in your Cat's mouth. Each successful kill earns 15 points, and when your Cat accumulates 100 points, it fills one bar (out of ten) on the Hunting panel.

Cat outside if gophers show up. Along with accumulating Hunting points, Cats improve their Fun and Hunger Motives when they track down a pest.

Cat mixing it up with an unsuspecting gopher.

When the dust settles, the gophers are gone and the harvest is safe.

NOTE

Stray Cats will also fight gophers, so don't be too eager to Shoo them off your property.

Cats also hunt gophers (in gardens), roaches, and rabbits (a civilized Sim would never allow his Cat to Hunt cottontails). They will not always wait for your Hunt command, which is a good thing if you have a garden. Cats are frequently running around the house while your Sim is sleeping, so instead of fast-forwarding to morning, you might want to keep an eye on the garden and send your

It's a Dog, Not a Hunter

Dogs do not Hunt in the true sense of the word, but they are useful for scaring off raccoons. Although raccoons appear harmless, they get into your garbage can and spread the contents all over the lawn and street. Dogs will fight with raccoons, and although they do not always win, when the tussle is over, the raccoons waddle away.

Naughty Pets

Aside from peeing on the floor or refusing to train, unhappy pets can be very destructive. If you let your Dog's Motives drop too low, don't be surprised to find holes all over your lawn. Your Sim can grab a hoe and fill in the damage, but this is time consuming. A few hugs and a full food dish go a long way to keeping your Dog happy and out of trouble.

Cats, especially strays, have a penchant for playing in garbage, a trait they share with raccoons. Keep tabs on your trash compactor and waste baskets to prevent your Sims from tossing garbage on the floor.

Playing with Your Pets

With all the Housebreaking and Training going on, it's easy to forget that pets require quality time with their owners. When a Dog or Cat is in a good Mood, the Play With menu is full, including Pet, Hug, Fetch, and Wrestle. Even if you forget to check your pet's Motives, you'll know when your pet is happy because you'll experience more random demonstrations of affection. A sure sign of a well-adjusted Dog is when both pet and owner flash "plus signs" when they come near each other.

NOTE

If your pet is out of sorts, there may be only one or two options on the Play With menu.

Hug

Pet

Fetch

Wrestle

Attack Pets

Well-trained Cats and Dogs will attack on command, and although the results are amusing, think twice about whom you target. The Attack menu includes the names of other Sims in the area, and all you need to do is select one to initiate the attack. Depending on your pet's Mood, this command can be ignored. However, if the pet is feeling frisky, it will seek out the attackee and tear into him or her, leaving the poor Sim frightened and confused.

This Cat can't even claw its way up to the table...not a good sign.

The worst part of a pet attack is the aftermath. The next time you approach a Sim whom you subjected to animal violence, you will get an understandably cool reception. So, if you're looking to make new friends while working on your next career promotion, attacking them with Fido is not a good idea.

Pet Shows

This show goes from bad to worse when the Cat scratches the judge.

After this performance, the only possible result for this mangy feline is a booby prize.

When you visit Sim Central Park with pets in tow, the Kennel Club President is all over you like a bad suit. You'll receive an invitation to enter the next show, and all it takes is §150 to gain admission. The Kennel Club does not make any determination of your pet's readiness, so you must decide whether or not you have a chance to earn an award.

Your chances for a positive outcome are increased if your pets Housebreaking, Hunting, Obedience, and Tricks Skills are at their maximum levels. However, your pet's current Mood is also very important. A well-trained pet will fall short of the 1st place ribbon if it is hungry, tired, or both (see the sidebar for details on scoring). Unless you just want to see your Cat or Dog abuse the judge, you'd best go home for some rest and relaxation, then return when your pet is feeling more positive about the world.

When your pet is impeccably trained and in a great Mood, the results are usually glorious. The animal hops obediently on the table, executes tricks on command, and doesn't even blink while the judge probes every available orifice.

A 1st place ribbon makes it all worthwhile! Your proud Sim takes the trophy home and places it in her brand-new §649 Crake's Cabinet.

PET SHOW POINT SYSTEM

The show judge totals all three pet Skills (Housebreaking/Hunting, Obedience, and Tricks). If the total Skill is above 2,250 (each bar on the Pet Skills panel is worth 100 points), and the pet's Mood is above 75, he awards 1st place. If the Mood is below 75, a 2nd place trophy is awarded. If the total skill is less than 2,250 but above 1,500, the prize is 3rd place. All totals under 1,500 earn an automatic booby prize.

The Maternity Box signals the arrival of puppies or kittens.

Breeding

It all starts with a snuggle.

Let's go somewhere more private.

If breeding animals was as hard in real life as it is in *The Sims Unleashed*, Dogs and Cats could roam free with no more worries about overpopulation. Setting the stage for two pets to like each other, snuggle down in the doghouse, and eventually make babies is a delicate process. The following list includes all the steps necessary to breed puppies or kittens.

1. **Bring two Dogs or two Cats home from Pet Paradise.**
2. **Nurture each pet and keep their Moods over 60.**
3. **Buy a doghouse and place it in a high-traffic area.**
4. **Keep both pets happy and watch their Short Term and Long Term Relationship scores (both must be over 50 to have a chance of "playing" together inside the doghouse).**
5. **If everything is perfect, and the two pets go into the doghouse together, there is only a one-in-fifteen chance they will produce a litter.**

After the babies arrive, you must focus on keeping the mother's Motives high for the next two days, during which time the babies mature into adults. If mom's Motives drop too low, you'll receive a warning from Animal Control. If the condition persists, they will come and whisk away the animals to a better home. If you decide to sell the new animals, their value is based on the combined qualities of the parents (Tricks and Obedience). The number of awards won by the parents is not figured into the equation.

Animal Control Officer

Aside from protecting the rights of puppies and kittens, the Animal Control Officer is ready, willing, and able to rid your home of furry pests, namely raccoons and skunks. In most cases, your Dog does an adequate job of keeping raccoons away, although the black-eyed invaders always arrive at night, and they are very noisy. If raccoons ignore your Dog, or even worse, kick its butt in a fight, you had better call Animal Control to remove the critter.

Skunks are another very stinky matter. A skunk may visit when your Hygiene drops below 30. It wanders around, and if it is left alone, you'll be no worse for the wear. However, if a Sim attempts to pet a skunk, or if one of your pets gets a little too inquisitive, the skunk will spray, dropping your Hygiene 100 points. After a visit, skunks will not return for four days.

CHAPTER 12:
BIRDS, FISH, TURTLES, AND IGUANAS

Although Dogs and Cats are the more known pets of *The Sims Unleashed* and the only animals that roam free, your Sims also enjoy owning object-based pets including Birds, Fish, Turtles, and Iguanas. Although these pets never leave their enclosures or perches, they interact with Sims and other animals, eat (if you remember to feed them), and require basic cleaning. You can even train Birds to talk (that is, if your Sim's intelligence transcends the level of a sparrow). Birds and goldfish also require a serious level of protection, because they qualify as a favorite source of entertainment and food for Sim Cats. In the following sections we introduce the "other" animals and offer tips on care, feeding, and interaction.

Lovebirds and Budgies

The Pet Paradise and Old Town Quarter sell a variety of lovebirds and budgies in the large

Birdcages against the far wall. Browse the Birdcages to get basic information on either breed.

You can also feed the parrots and cockatoos while you're here. They aren't for sale in the

shops, but if you like them, you can go home and purchase one in Buy Mode from the Pet menu.

If you decide to buy lovebirds or budgies, take your selection to the cashier. Your purchase is placed in your Inventory, and when you return home, you can buy Birdcages for your feathered friends from the Pet menu.

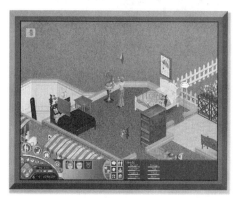

The small Birdcage fits neatly on a table. Click on the Birdcage to "Add" your Bird. When it is happily chirping inside the Birdcage, you can click on it and select View, Feed, or Play With. Playing with the Birds increases your Sim's Fun score. But you must take time out from fun and games to

clean the Birdcage. A dirty Birdcage won't kill your Birds, but it degrades the Room score, and the smell attracts flies after about six hours.

CAUTION

Overfeeding is a common problem with object-based pets. There is no obvious indication of how much your pet is eating, and the Feed option stays on the menu all the time, so feed each pet only once per day. This will keep them alive and healthy without risking overfeeding and sudden death. Small Birds will chirp a lot when they are hungry, and parrots and cockatoos will bellow when hungry.

TIP

When placing a large Birdcage, make sure your Sims can access its front door. You can inadvertently place the Birdcage against a wall, thereby preventing the Sims from feeding or playing with the Birds.

Cats have a special love for Birds, especially when they are hungry and in a bad mood. If you don't pay attention, the family Cat will check out the Birdcage from below, climb up to the table, then reach in and grab the Birds. In a few quick bites, your lovable Cat satisfies Hunger and Fun Motives. Obviously, losing your Birds to a violent death is a traumatic experience. And, adding insult to injury, Cats continue to receive Fun points while pawing an empty Birdcage. Cats only go after Birds in small Birdcages, so if you have the simoleans for a big Birdcage, you won't have to worry. Cats will still climb onto the large cage and paw at the Birds, but because that cage is fairly large, the Birds can easily avoid the Cats' paws.

If you want to enjoy your Birds, you'd better keep tabs on your tabby. It takes a while for the Cat to grab the Birds after it climbs onto the Birdcage, so you have time to Shoo the cat away, buying a reprieve for your defenseless Birds.

NOTE

Select the Birdcage, not the Cat, to access the Shoo command.

Your best defense against lethal Cat attacks is to make sure your cat's Hunger Motive is satisfied, and that the pet food dish is full before you go to bed. Doing this guards against your Cat looking for a midnight snack while your Sims are snoozing. However, don't be surprised if your cat passes up the kibble for Bird even when the food dish is full.

CAUTION

Although it may be tempting to place the Birdcage in your Sim's bedroom so you can quickly intercept the Cat, this is a bad idea. Your Sims will not sleep well with the Bird chirping all night. Instead, place the Birdcage close to, but not in, the bedroom.

Parrots and Cockatoos

As you tour Old Town, you have the opportunity to feed or chat with parrots and cockatoos. The experiences can be fun, frustrating, or painful, depending on the Bird's mood. If you want the big Birds in your home, you can obtain them in Buy Mode. Both Birds come fully equipped with perches and food cups, so all you need to do is add love and seed.

Having Fun with Your Talking Bird

Unlike budgies and lovebirds, where your only activities are Fill Food and Play With, parrots and cockatoos offer four options: Fill Food, Dance, Talk, and Feed Cracker. As with the other Birds, select Fill Food only once a day to avoid overfeeding and eventually killing your pet. Choose Feed Cracker when your Sim is in a good mood, or the Bird is likely to take a nip of flesh along with the munchie.

Cleaning Up the Droppings

Aside from feeding and cleaning (more on this later), you can train your parrot or cockatoo to talk and dance. Each time your Sim completes a successful training session, you earn a Charisma skill point. Training success is dependent upon the existing Charisma skill of the Sim and the abilities of the Bird. So, a smart parrot trained by a charismatic Sim produces the fastest and most positive results, but a newly acquired cockatoo trained by a Sim with no Charisma takes longer.

Big Birds make big messes. Although a parrot or cockatoo won't expire from a messy perch, it does little to enhance your Room score, and eventually it breeds flies or mice (if you have a Cat). The maid will clean, but jump in with a mop if the flies start buzzing.

NOTE

Children do not earn Charisma points, but they receive a Fun boost when training a Bird. The success of a training session is affected by a Sim-kid's school grades. Better grades translate to faster training.

When Polly Goes Belly Up

Overfeeding your parrot or cockatoo results in tragedy. A Sim will mourn a dead Bird, but don't let the grieving go on too long; the corpse degrades your Room score.

Fish

When you buy Fish at Pet Paradise, they are added to your Sim's Inventory. Purchase a Fish Bowl in Buy Mode when you return from the store. After adding the Fish, feed them once a day, clean the bowl when it is dirty, and Shoo the Cat away when it has a taste for seafood. Cats are relentless when it comes to seafood, so keep your pet's food dish full to prevent your Cat from eating elsewhere.

NOTE

Cats watch Fish and Birds for Fun. They will eat Fish and Birds if they are hungry and in a bad mood. If the Cats are happy, they will not eat the Birds.

Turtles

Turtles are easier to care for than Fish, because you don't have to worry about the cat. And, you have the added benefit of nuzzling your Turtle. Turtle enclosures and Fish Bowls are small, so keep them on the same table. This way, you can feed the turtle and Shoo the cat away from the Fish without having to run across the room.

Iguanas

At §199, Iguanas are more expensive than Turtles or Fish, and their enclosures set you back §879. However, Iguanas do not make noise, so you can keep them in your bedroom. The inhabited Terrarium adds four points to both your Fun and Room scores. Like the other object-based pets, you must regularly feed and clean Iguanas, but you don't have to worry about the cat.

CHAPTER 13:
NEW CAREERS

Introduction

The *Sims Unleashed* adds five new career tracks for your Sims: Fashion, Education, Animal Care, Culinary, and Circus. This chapter includes job descriptions and promotion requirements for all 10 levels of each new career. We begin with a little career counseling to help you choose a job to fit your Sim's personality.

Career Choices

CAREER TRACK	CRITICAL SKILLS	RELATED PERSONALITY TRAITS
Fashion	Charisma, Body, Creativity	Outgoing, Active, Playful
Education	Logic, Creativity, Charisma	Outgoing, Playful
Animal Care	Charisma, Body, Logic	Outgoing, Active
Culinary	Cooking, Charisma	Outgoing
Circus	Charisma, Body, Creativity	Outgoing, Active, Playful

Sim Career Tracks

The following tables list the salaries, hours, car pool vehicles, and job level requirements for the five new career tracks in *The Sims Unleashed*. Sims are paid daily. Also listed is the daily decay rate for each motive when the Sim is at work.

Requirements for Level 1 Positions

CAREER TRACK	POSITION	PAY	HOURS	CAR POOL VEHICLE	COOKING	REPAIR	CHARISMA	BODY	LOGIC	CREATIVITY	FAMILY/ FRIENDS	DAILY MOTIVE DECAY (HUNGER/COMFORT/ HYGIENE/BLADDER/ ENERGY/FUN/SOCIAL)
Fashion	Dept. Store Clerk	§130	9 a.m.–3 p.m.	Junker	0	0	0	0	0	0	0	0/0/0/0/-30/0/0
Education	Playground Monitor	§120	7 a.m.–1 p.m.	Junker	0	0	0	0	0	0	0	0/0/0/0/-30/0/0
Animal Care	Dog Walker	§100	1 p.m.–3 p.m.	Junker	0	0	0	0	0	0	0	0/0/0/0/-30/5/0
Culinary	Dishwasher	§90	6 a.m.–12 p.m.	Junker	0	0	0	0	0	0	0	0/0/0/0/-30/0/0
Circus	Popcorn Vendor	§90	4 p.m.–11 p.m.	Junker	0	0	0	0	0	0	0	0/-5/0/0/-25/0/0

Requirements for Level 2 Positions

CAREER TRACK	POSITION	PAY	HOURS	CAR POOL VEHICLE	COOKING	REPAIR	CHARISMA	BODY	LOGIC	CREATIVITY	FAMILY/ FRIENDS	DAILY MOTIVE DECAY (HUNGER/COMFORT/ HYGIENE/BLADDER/ ENERGY/FUN/SOCIAL)
Fashion	Tailor	§190	9 a.m.–3 p.m.	Std. Car	0	0	0	0	0	0	0	0/0/0/0/-30/0/0
Education	Substitute Teacher	§180	7 a.m.–1 p.m.	Junker	0	0	0	0	0	0	0	0/0/-12/0/-20/0/0
Animal Care	Pet Groomer	§160	9 a.m.–3 p.m.	Truck	0	0	0	0	0	0	0	0/0/0/0/-30/0/0
Culinary	Drive Thru Order Taker	§120	5 a.m.–10 a.m.	Truck	0	0	0	0	0	0	0	0/0/0/0/-30/0/0
Circus	Ticket Taker	§130	3 p.m.–6 p.m.	Junker	0	0	0	0	0	0	0	0/10/0/0/-10/0/0

Requirements for Level 3 Positions

CAREER TRACK	POSITION	PAY	HOURS	CAR POOL VEHICLE	COOKING	REPAIR	CHARISMA	BODY	LOGIC	CREATIVITY	FAMILY/ FRIENDS	DAILY MOTIVE DECAY (HUNGER/COMFORT/ HYGIENE/BLADDER/ ENERGY/FUN/SOCIAL)
Fashion	Makeup Artist	§210	9 a.m.–3 p.m.	Std. Car	0	0	1	0	0	1	1	0/0/0/0/-36/0/0
Education	Kindergarten Teacher	§190	7 a.m.–1 p.m.	Junker	1	0	0	0	0	1	1	0/0/-12/0/-36/0/0
Animal Care	Sheep Custodian	§185	9 a.m.–3 p.m.	Truck	1	0	2	0	0	0	1	0/0/0/0/-35/0/0
Culinary	Fast Food Shift Manager	§130	9 a.m.–3 p.m.	Truck	2	0	0	0	0	0	0	0/0/0/0/-35/0/0
Circus	Midway Carnie	§140	3 p.m.–12 a.m.	Junker	0	1	1	1	0	0	0	0/0/-16/0/-36/0/0

Requirements for Level 4 Positions

CAREER TRACK	POSITION	PAY	HOURS	CAR POOL VEHICLE	COOKING	REPAIR	CHARISMA	BODY	LOGIC	CREATIVITY	FAMILY/ FRIENDS	DAILY MOTIVE DECAY (HUNGER/COMFORT/ HYGIENE/BLADDER/ ENERGY/FUN/SOCIAL)
Fashion	Painter's Model	§235	12 p.m.–3 p.m.	Std. Car	1	0	2	1	0	1	1	0/0/-9/0/-36/0/0
Education	Junior High School Teacher	§210	8 a.m.–3 p.m.	Std. Car	1	0	1	0	1	1	2	0/0/-9/0/-36/0/0
Animal Care	Aquarium Technician	§250	12 p.m.–5 p.m.	Truck	1	1	2	1	0	1	1	-7/-7/-7/0/-35/0/0
Culinary	Sous Chef	§180	9 a.m.–3 p.m.	Std. Car	3	2	0	0	0	0	1	0/0/-9/0/-36/0/0
Circus	Sideshow Barker	§180	3 p.m.–10 p.m.	Circus Truck	0	1	1	2	0	1	1	-7/-7/-7/0/-35/0/0

Requirements for Level 5 Positions

CAREER TRACK	POSITION	PAY	HOURS	CAR POOL VEHICLE	COOKING	REPAIR	CHARISMA	BODY	LOGIC	CREATIVITY	FAMILY/ FRIENDS	DAILY MOTIVE DECAY (HUNGER/COMFORT/ HYGIENE/BLADDER/ ENERGY/FUN/SOCIAL)
Fashion	Fashion Photographer	§450	11 a.m.–4 p.m.	SUV	1	1	2	1	0	2	2	-7/0/-14/0/-42/-7/0
Education	High School Teacher	§290	8 a.m.–3 p.m.	Std. Car	1	0	2	0	3	2	2	-7/0/-14/0/-42/-7/0
Animal Care	Zoo Keeper	§345	6 a.m.–12 p.m.	SUV	2	1	3	1	0	1	2	-6/0/-24/0/-54/0/0
Culinary	Head Chef	§220	9 a.m.–3 p.m.	Std. Car	6	2	2	0	0	2	3	-6/0/-12/0/-42/-6/0
Circus	Clown	§200	4 p.m.–1 p.m.	Clown Car	0	1	2	4	0	1	4	-7/0/-14/0/-42/-7/0

Requirements for Level 6 Positions

CAREER TRACK	POSITION	PAY	HOURS	CAR POOL VEHICLE	COOKING	REPAIR	CHARISMA	BODY	LOGIC	CREATIVITY	FAMILY/ FRIENDS	DAILY MOTIVE DECAY (HUNGER/COMFORT/ HYGIENE/BLADDER/ ENERGY/FUN/SOCIAL)
Fashion	Tradeshow Model	§600	5 p.m.–1 a.m.	Town Car	1	1	4	3	0	4	3	-8/0/-16/0/-48/-8/0
Education	Principal	§310	8 a.m.–3 p.m.	Std. Car	1	0	3	0	5	3	3	-14/0/-14/0/-49/-7/0
Animal Care	Dolphin Trainer	§435	11 a.m.–4 p.m.	SUV	2	2	4	2	1	1	2	-12/0/-30/0/-60/0/0
Culinary	Restaurant Critic	§335	3 p.m.–11 p.m.	Std. Car	6	3	4	0	0	3	3	-9/0/-9/0/-45/-9/0
Circus	Human Cannonball	§240	9 a.m.–3 p.m.	Circus Truck	0	1	4	5	1	1	5	-12/0/-30/0/-60/0/0

Requirements for Level 7 Positions

CAREER TRACK	POSITION	PAY	HOURS	CAR POOL VEHICLE	COOKING	REPAIR	CHARISMA	BODY	LOGIC	CREATIVITY	FAMILY/ FRIENDS	DAILY MOTIVE DECAY (HUNGER/COMFORT/ HYGIENE/BLADDER/ ENERGY/FUN/SOCIAL)
Fashion	Runway Model	§650	1 p.m.–10 p.m.	Town Car	1	1	6	5	0	5	4	-15/0/-20/0/-45/-10/-1(
Education	Assistant Professor	§490	9 a.m.–6 p.m.	Std. Car	1	0	4	0	6	5	4	-15/0/-20/0/-45/-10/-1(
Animal Care	Animal Acting Coach	§560	9 a.m.–3 p.m.	SUV	2	2	5	3	2	2	4	-14/0/-35/0/-63/0/0
Culinary	Cook Book Author	§580	3 p.m.–11 p.m.	Std. Car	8	4	5	0	0	4	5	-18/0/-24/0/-54/-12/0
Circus	Acrobat	§500	4 p.m.–11 p.m.	Circus Truck	0	1	5	6	2	4	6	-14/0/-35/0/-63/0/0

Requirements for Level 8 Positions

CAREER TRACK	POSITION	PAY	HOURS	CAR POOL VEHICLE	COOKING	REPAIR	CHARISMA	BODY	LOGIC	CREATIVITY	FAMILY/ FRIENDS	DAILY MOTIVE DECAY (HUNGER/COMFORT/ HYGIENE/BLADDER/ ENERGY/FUN/SOCIAL)
Fashion	Supermodel	§875	11 a.m.–4 p.m.	Town Car	1	1	8	7	0	6	5	-16/0/-24/0/-56/-16/0
Education	Tenured Professor	§600	9 a.m.–5 p.m.	Town Car	1	0	6	0	8	7	5	-20/0/-40/0/-70/-5/0
Animal Care	Alligator Relocator	§700	2 p.m.–9 p.m.	SUV	3	3	6	5	3	3	4	-20/0/-40/0/-70/-5/0
Culinary	Restaurateur	§690	9 a.m.–2 p.m.	Town Car	8	4	7	0	0	5	6	-20/0/-25/0/-50/-10/-1(
Circus	Trapeze Artist	§610	4 p.m.–11 p.m.	Circus Truck	0	3	6	7	2	5	6	-20/0/-40/0/-70/-5/0

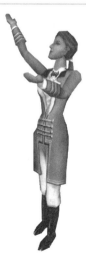

Requirements for Level 9 Positions

CAREER TRACK	POSITION	PAY	HOURS	CAR POOL VEHICLE	COOKING	REPAIR	CHARISMA	BODY	LOGIC	CREATIVITY	FAMILY/ FRIENDS	DAILY MOTIVE DECAY (HUNGER/COMFORT/ HYGIENE/BLADDER/ ENERGY/FUN/SOCIAL)
Fashion	Fashion Columnist	§1,050	5 p.m.–12 a.m.	Bentley	1	1	10	9	0	7	6	-21/0/-35/0/-56/-21/0
Education	College Dean	§700	9 a.m.–3 p.m.	Limo	1	0	6	0	9	9	7	-24/0/-28/0/-56/-16/-16
Animal Care	Veterinarian	§780	8 a.m.–3 p.m.	Town Car	4	4	7	5	5	4	5	-21/0/-35/0/-56/-21/0
Culinary	Celebrity Chef	§760	3 p.m.–11 p.m.	Town Car	10	4	8	0	0	5	9	-21/0/-35/0/-56/-21/0
Circus	Lion Tamer	§775	4 p.m.–11 p.m.	Circus Truck	1	3	8	8	3	5	7	-24/0/-42/0/-72/-6/0

Requirements for Level 10 Positions

CAREER TRACK	POSITION	PAY	HOURS	CAR POOL VEHICLE	COOKING	REPAIR	CHARISMA	BODY	LOGIC	CREATIVITY	FAMILY/ FRIENDS	DAILY MOTIVE DECAY (HUNGER/COMFORT/ HYGIENE/BLADDER/ ENERGY/FUN/SOCIAL)
Fashion	Fashion Designer	§1,350	4 p.m.–11 p.m.	Bentley	1	1	10	10	0	8	7	-30/0/-40/0/-65/-25/0
Education	Minister of Education	§900	10 a.m.–5 p.m.	Limo	1	0	6	0	10	10	9	-30/0/-36/0/-66/-24/0
Animal Care	Animal Magician	§1,050	6 p.m.–12 a.m.	Limo	4	5	9	6	6	5	8	-30/0/-40/0/-65/-25/0
Culinary	Candy Bar Magnate	§930	4 p.m.–11 p.m.	Limo	10	5	10	0	0	6	11	-30/0/-36/0/-66/-24/0
Circus	Ringmaster	§815	5 p.m.–11 p.m.	Clown Car	1	3	9	8	5	6	8	-30/0/-40/0/-65/-25/0

CHAPTER 14:
NEW OBJECTS

The Sims Unleashed presents more than 125 new items, including 30 new pet and garden objects available in Buy Mode, and a variety of park, market, café bar, and shopping objects for the new Community Lots. You'll also find new spiral staircases, and a stylish new French Quarter collection of walls, floor, doors, windows, furniture, and decorations (see the Build Mode section at the end of this chapter). The objects are arranged by category, as they appear on the Buy Mode menus (Seating, Surfaces, Decorative, etc.) with pictures, prices, and ratings (if applicable). The Efficiency Value (1-10) indicates how well an item satisfies its related Motive, with a higher number being worth more to your Sims. Objects available only on the Community Lot Buy Mode menus are listed in a separate section.

SEATING

Chairs

Anchor Lace Café

Cost: §389

Motive: Comfort (3), Room (2)

The Occasional Chaisonal

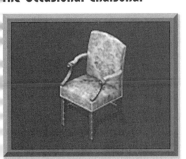

Cost: §411

Motive: Comfort (5)

Sofas

Cast Iron Comfort Loveseat

Cost: §399

Motives: Comfort (2), Room (1)

Poissons De Vol Café Sofa

Cost: §699

Motives: Comfort (7), Energy (4)

SURFACES

Counters

Laika's Counter

Cost: §139

Motive: N/A

"Piece of the Pie" Garden Counter

Cost: §209

Motive: N/A

Lonely Oak Café Counter

Cost: §335

Motive: N/A

Tables
The Plank

Cost: §169

Motive: N/A

Table Ferme

Cost: §269

Motive: N/A

Monsieur Fer Table

Cost: §369

Motives: Room (1)

Ordure Café Coffee Table

Cost: §549

Motives: Room (2)

DECORATIVE

Paintings

Spunky Junky Cat Nip Advertisement

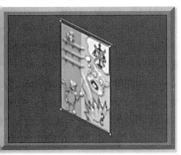

Cost: §70

Motive: Room (1)

Furry Serf

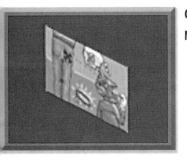

Cost: §133

Motive: Room (1)

Antique Poster

Cost: §449

Motive: Room (3)

RandImage Café Decoration

Cost: §1,333

Motive: Room (4)

Sculptures

"The Power of Heeling"

Cost: §733

Motives: Room (3)

Other

Poetry in Motion Fountain

Cost: §39

Motives: Fun (2)

Notes: For Sims and their pets

Futilo Bronze Windchime

Cost: §60

Motives: Room (1)

Clevergreen Fabric Awning

Cost: §68

Motive: N/A

Shutters Provencal

Cost: §80

Motive: N/A

Horse Head Hitching Post

Cost: §88

Motives: N/A

Geranium Flower Stand

Cost: §89

Motive: N/A

Neo Grec Window Dressing

Cost: §99

Motive: N/A

Steve the Happy Scarecrow

Cost: §125

Motives: N/A

Notes: Limits gopher destruction

urinal Fire Plug

Cost: §130

Motive: N/A

loak of Protection

Cost: §155

Motive: N/A

Neptune's Sorrow Iron Fountain

Cost: §2,999

Motive: Room (4)

APPLIANCES
Refrigerators
Never Cold Food Hold

Cost: §299

Motive: Hunger (5)

Pantry De Provence

Cost: §899

Motive: Hunger (7)

PLUMBING
Showers/Tubs
Fontleroy Shower Tub

Cost: §715

Motives: Comfort (1), Hygiene (5)

Other
RepublicClean Toilet Stall

Cost: §550

Motives: Bladder (8)

LIGHTING
Table Lamps
Licentious Luminance Parlor Lamp

Cost: §235

Motive: Room (1)

Wall Lamps
Bohemian Glow Sconce

Cost: §319

Motive: Room (1)

Hanging Lamps
The "No Rustle" Ceiling Fan

Cost: §329

Motive: Room (2)

Other
Ye Olde 20th Century Banners

Cost: §1,100

Motive: N/A

MISCELLANEOUS
Pets
Classic Goldfish Bowl

Cost: §35

Motive: Fun (1), Room (1)

et PlaCater

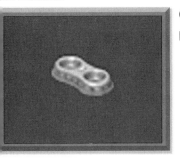

Cost: §45

Motive: Hunger (6)

cratcheriffic Scratching Post

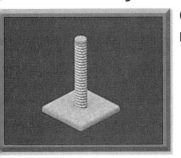

Cost: §59

Motive: Fun (5)

ove in a Cage

Cost: §65

Motive: Room (1), Fun (2)

ura-Bean Pet Bed

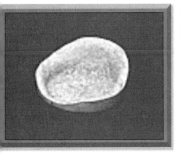

Cost: §75

Motive: Comfort (6), Energy (6)

Timid Turtle Action Playset

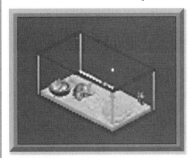

Cost: §89

Motives: Room (2), Fun (2)

Notes: Group activity

Annapurna Pet Feeder

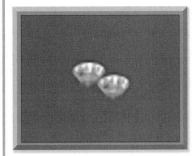

Cost: §119

Motive: Hunger (8)

Dunginator 9000

Cost: §139

Motive: Bladder (8)

Happy Paws Cuddle Sack

Cost: §175

Motive: Comfort (7), Energy (7)

Critter Condo

Cost: §245

Motive: Comfort (6), Energy (6)

Shag Spyer

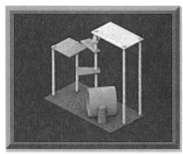

Cost: §299

Motive: Comfort (4), Energy (6)

Persian Plush Pet Bed

Cost: §349

Motive: Comfort (8), Energy (9)

Squeak-EE-Clean Pet Tub

Cost: §349

Motive: Comfort (3), Hygiene (7)

Pad Prolifique

Cost: §599

Motive: Comfort (9), Energy (9)

Crake's Cabinet

Cost: §649

Motive: Room (3)

Description: Holds Pet Show awards

r. Beau

Cost: §749

Motive: Increases Charisma Skill

Notes: Includes cockatoo, perch, and food cup

rgotten Jungle Terrarium

Cost: §879

Motive: Room (4), Fun (4)

eaky Scarlet

Cost: §939

Motives: Increases Charisma Skill

Notes: Includes parrot, perch, and food cup

line Funinator

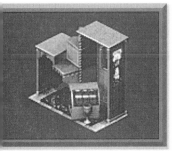

Cost: §999

Motive: Comfort (5), Energy (7)

The Aviary

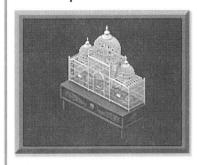

Cost: §1,299

Motive: Room (4), Fun (2)

COMMUNITY LOT OBJECTS

Food

Decorative

Inner Beast Mask

Cost: §35

Motive: N/A

The Rage Mask

Cost: §69

Motive: Room (1)

"Get Your Crack On" Café sign

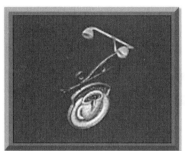

Cost: §99

Motive: N/A

Produce Market Shingle

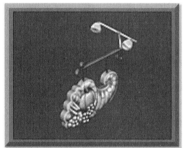

Cost: §99

Motive: N/A

The Subvert Mask

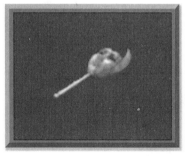

Cost: §111

Motive: Room (1)

The Rememberer Mask

Cost: §159

Motive: Room (1)

Electronics
Screaming Buttress Wall Speaker

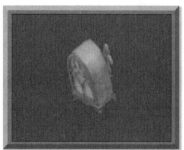

Cost: §459

Motive: N/A

Appliances
Vegano Market Cart

Cost: §1,984

Motives: N/A

Notes: Sims can buy veggies at this cart Prices range from §7–§45

"Pasticcetera" Pastry Cart

Cost: §4,700

Motive: Hunger (4)

Notes: Pastry costs §

avelin' Joe's Espresso Bar

Cost: §4,900

Motive: Hunger (3)

Notes: Coffee costs §12

Salamander Rising

Cost: §89

Motive: Room (1)

ops

ectronics

echanique Cash Register

Cost: §275

Motive: N/A

Blackened Brightlight

Cost: §135

Motive: Room (1)

ghting

Wick Sage

Cost: §55

Motive: N/A

Spooky Skull

Cost: §200

Motive: Room (2)

Miscellaneous
Magic Beans Counter

Cost: §599

Motive: N/A

Notes: Seeds cost §15–25

The Collar Purple

Cost: §699

Motive: N/A

Notes: Display contains cat collars and ribbons (ribbons are the same price as the corresponding collar). The items are priced as follows: Pink §15, Brown §16, Blue §18, Red §19; Spiked collar is §25.

Praisem High Pet Treat Display

Cost: §799

Motive: N/A

Notes: Pet treat costs §40

Canine Collar Contraption

Cost: §1,099

Motive: N/A

Notes: Display contains dog collar and ribbons (ribbons are the same price as the corresponding collar). The items are priced as follows: Pink §15, Brown §16, Blue §18, Red §19; Spiked collar is §25.

Auntie Esther's Seeds

Cost: §1,199

Motive: N/A

Notes: Seeds are priced as follows: R Mater Tomato Seed §15, "Lean 'N' Mean" Green Bean §18, "Get Ahead" Lettuce Seeds §20, and Money Bunny Carrot Seeds §25.

SqueakNip Pet Toys

Cost: §1,739

Motive: N/A

Notes: Marty McMousenip costs §45, Squeaky Sara §25, and Gnawhide §49

Ornitharium Bird Display

Cost: §3,399

Motive: N/A

Notes: Budgies cost §35, Lovebirds §59

Shallow Tallow Candle Displays

Cost: §3,499

Motive: N/A

Notes: Candle prices are as follows: Big Wick Sage Candle §55, Salamander Rising Candle §89, Blackened Brightlight Candle §135, and Spooky Skull Candle §200

Aquaversatile Pet Display

Cost: §3,899

Motive: N/A

Notes: Fish cost §15

Stacked Box Display Case

Cost: §4,199

Motive: N/A

Notes: Turtles cost §99

Grand Delusions Mask Display

Cost: §5,888

Motive: N/A

Notes: The Rememberer mask costs §159, Subvert §111, Inner Beast §35, and Rage §69; all masks except Inner Beast (0) add Room (1)

Frisky Feline Promo Pen

Cost: §6998

Motive: N/A

Notes: Sims pay §399 to adopt a cat

Fluffy Puppy Pet Bin

Cost: §6999

Motive: N/A

Notes: Sims pay §399 to adopt a dog

Outdoors
Decorative
CandleLodge Deceptivator

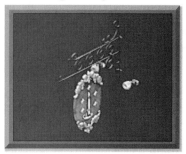

Cost: §99
Motive: N/A

Pet on a Shingle

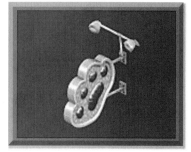

Cost: §99
Motive: N/A

Electronics
Fancee Phone

Cost: §551
Motive: N/A

Miscellaneous
Fancy Fur Pet Judging Station

Cost: §199
Motives: N/A

Rompin' Bronco

Cost: §235
Motive: Fun (4)

Ceti the Happy Whale

Cost: §245
Motive: Fun (4)

Gravpacto Trash Plunger

Cost: §329
Motives: N/A

Pet's Potential Play Palace

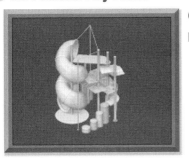

Cost: §2,099

Motives: Fun (7)

BUILD MODE
Wall and Fence Tool
Fence Zilbert

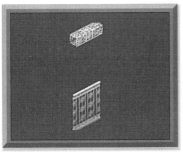

Cost: §149

Motive: N/A

Arch Zilbert

Cost: §199

Motive: N/A

Fence de la Nuit

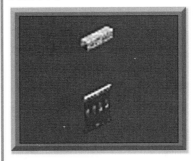

Cost: §199

Motive: N/A

Brickwick Security Fencing

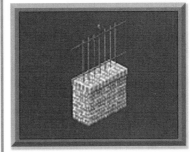

Cost: §239

Motive: N/A

Arch de la Nuit

Cost: §255

Motive: N/A

Stair Tool

Pallid Ascension

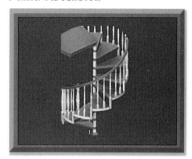

Cost: §1,300

Motives: N/A

Woodwind Genome

Cost: §1,999

Motives: N/A

Cast Iron Spiral Staircase

Cost: §2,499

Motives: N/A

Plant Tool

Insta-Plot Victory Garden

Cost: §65

Motive: N/A

Jasminum Permatrellisium

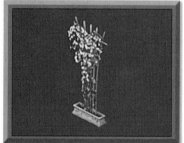

Cost: §135

Motive: N/A

W-235 Willow

Cost: §400

Motives: N/A

Sycamore

Cost: §305

Motives: N/A

Door Tools

French Burgundy

Cost: §160

Motive: N/A

Mary's Last Defense

Cost: §210

Motive: N/A

Mais Oui Café Door

Cost: §373

Motive: N/A

Windows

Taponda Glass Window

Cost: §63

Motives: N/A

Mais Oui Café Window

Cost: §145

Motives: N/A

Franken Belly Window

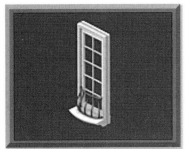

Cost: §185

Motives: N/A

CHAPTER 15:
INTERACTION TABLES

Introduction

The following tables contain relevant data for every interaction in *The Sims Unleashed*, including Short Term and Long Term Relationships. The interactions are broken down into four sections: adult to adult, adult to child, child to adult, and child to child. Each section contains three tables. The first table describes the general requirements for a successful interaction, and the second lists the effects of all possible results of each interaction. The third lists the conditions that determine whether or not a specific interaction shows up as an option in your menus. Use these tables to gauge your chance of success with each interaction.

Adult-to-Adult Interactions

Key	
>	Greater than
≥	Greater than or equal to
<	Less than
≤	Less than or equal to

Adult Interaction Success Requirements

CATEGORY	INTERACTION	INITIATOR REQUIREMENTS	RECIPIENT REQUIREMENTS
Ask	How Are You?	None	Mood ≥ -80
	How's Work?	None	Mood ≥ -30
	Invite Downtown	None	Energy ≥ 0, Daily ≥ -20
	Invite Home	None	Mood ≥ 40, Outgoing > 9
		None	Mood ≥ 40, Lifetime > 50
		None	Mood ≥ 40, Daily ≥ 55, Outgoing > 5
		None	Mood ≥ 40, Daily ≥ 70
	Let's Hang Out/Date	Hygiene > -10	Daily > 10
	Move In	None	Lifetime ≥ 60, Mood ≥ 45, Daily ≥ 85
	Propose	Different Genders	Love, Lifetime > 80, Daily > 75, Mood > 60
	What Are You Into?	None	Mood ≥ -30
Attack	Fight	Body ≥ Recipient's Body	None
	Shove	Body ≥ Recipient's Body +2	None
	Slap	Body > Recipient's Body	None
	Slap Fight	None	Daily ≥ 20, Mood ≥ 10, Playful ≥ 6
Brag	Boast	None	Daily between 0 and 25, Mood > 10
	Flex	None	Nice ≥ 9
		Body > Recipient's Body +5	None
		None	Daily ≥ 30
		None	Mood ≥ 25
	Primp	None	Daily ≥ 50
		None	Daily > 0, Outgoing > 6
		None	Daily > 0, Mood ≥ 35

Adult Interaction Success Requirements, continued

CATEGORY	INTERACTION	INITIATOR REQUIREMENTS	RECIPIENT REQUIREMENTS
Cheer Up	Comfort	None	Daily ≥ 65
		None	Daily > 55, Outgoing ≤ 3
	Encourage	None	Outgoing > 7
		None	Mood ≥ -25
	With Puppet	None	Playful > 7
		None	Nice ≥ 4, Mood ≥ -30
		None	Nice < 4, Mood ≥ -40
Compliment	Admire	None	Nice ≤ 3, Mood > 60
		None	Nice > 3, Daily > -25
		None	Nice > 3, Mood > 10
	Worship	None	Daily ≥ 20, Charisma ≥ 7
		None	Daily ≥ 20, Outgoing ≤ 3, Mood > 60
		None	Daily ≥ 20, Outgoing > 3, Nice > 4
		None	Daily ≥ 20, Outgoing > 3, Nice ≤ 3, Mood > 60
Dance	Lively	None	Daily > -10, Energy ≥ 10, Mood ≥ 0, Outgoing > 3
		None	Daily > -10, Energy ≥ 10, Mood ≥ 0, Outgoing ≤ 3, Mood > 40
		None	Daily > -10, Energy ≥ 10, Mood ≥ 0, Outgoing ≤ 3, Daily > 30
	Slow	Hygiene > 20	Energy > 10, Mood > 20, Daily > -10, Outgoing > 3
		Hygiene > 20	Energy > 10, Mood > 20, Daily > -10, Lifetime ≥ 35
		Hygiene > 20	Energy > 10, Mood > 40, Outgoing ≤ 3
		Hygiene > 20	Energy > 10, Mood > 20, Daily > 30, Lifetime ≥ 35

Adult Interaction Success Requirements, continued

CATEGORY	INTERACTION	INITIATOR REQUIREMENTS	RECIPIENT REQUIREMENTS
Entertain	Joke	None	Playful > 7
		None	Playful < 3, Daily > 30
		None	Playful ≥ 3, Mood > 50, Daily > 30
	(Mild Accept)	None	Playful ≥ 3, Daily < -10
	(Mild Accept)	None	Playful < 3, Mood > 50, Daily < -10
	Juggle	None	Playful > 7
		None	Playful ≥ 3, Daily > 20
		None	Playful < 3, Mood > 50, Daily > 20
	With Puppet	None	Nice < 4, Mood > 50
		None	Nice ≥ 3, Playful ≥ 7
		None	Nice ≥ 3, Playful < 3, Mood > 50
Flirt	Check Out	None	Mood ≥ -10, Outgoing ≥ 7
		None	Mood ≥ -10, Outgoing > 2, Mood > 40
		None	Mood ≥ -10, Outgoing > 2, Daily > 20
		None	Mood ≥ -10, Outgoing ≤ 2, Charisma ≥ 3
		None	Mood ≥ -10, Outgoing ≤ 2, Body ≥ 5
		None	Mood ≥ -10, Outgoing ≤ 2, Mood > 30
		None	Mood ≥ -10, Outgoing ≤ 2, Daily > 15
	Growl	None	Mood ≥ 20, Outgoing ≥ 9
		None	Mood < 20, Lifetime ≥ 30
		None	Outgoing ≥ 4
		None	Mood > 50
		None	Daily > 25
	Back Rub	None	Mood > 20, Daily or Lifetime > 35
		None	Mood > 20, Outgoing ≥ 6
		None	Mood > 20, Daily > 30
	Sweet Talk	None	Daily or Lifetime ≥ 40
Greet	Wave	None	Lifetime > -40
	Shake Hands	None	Lifetime ≥ -20
	Air Kiss	None	Lifetime ≥ 20
	Kiss Cheek	None	Lifetime ≥ 20
	Hug	None	Lifetime > -20
	Romantic Kiss	None	Lifetime ≥ 50
		In Love	In Love
	Suave Kiss	None	Lifetime > 15

Adult Interaction Success Requirements, continued

CATEGORY	INTERACTION	INITIATOR REQUIREMENTS	RECIPIENT REQUIREMENTS
Hug	Friendly	Hygiene ≥ -40	Mood > 50
		Hygiene ≥ -40	Daily > 30
		Hygiene ≥ -40	Nice ≥ 2, Mood > 10
	Intimate	Hygiene ≥ -40	Nice ≥ 3, Daily > 20
		Hygiene ≥ -40	Nice < 3, Mood > 60
		Hygiene ≥ -40	Nice < 3, Daily or Lifetime > 30
	Leap into Arms	Hygiene ≥ -40	Nice or Playful ≥ 7
		Hygiene ≥ -40	Mood > 40
		Hygiene ≥ -40	Daily > 45
		Hygiene ≥ -40	Lifetime > 30
	Romantic	Hygiene ≥ -40	Nice < 3, Mood > 60
		Hygiene ≥ -40	Nice < 3, Daily > 50
		Hygiene ≥ -40	Nice < 3, Lifetime > 40
		Hygiene ≥ -40	Nice ≥ 3, Daily > 30
		Hygiene ≥ -40	Nice ≥ 3, Lifetime > 35
Insult	Shake Fist	None	Nice ≥ 4, -30 < Mood < 0
		None	Nice ≥ 4, Mood > 0, Daily ≤ 20
	Poke	None	Nice < 4
		None	Nice ≥ 4, Mood ≤ 0
		None	Nice ≥ 4, Mood > 0, Daily < 20
Kiss	Peck	None	Mood > 0, Lifetime ≥ 10, Daily ≥ 20
		None	Mood > 0, Daily ≥ 20
	Polite	None	Daily ≥ 20, Lifetime > 10, Mood ≥ 25
	Suave	None	Mood >0, Lifetime ≥ 15, Daily ≥ 30
	Romantic	None	Crush
		None	Daily > 60, Mood > 40
		None	Lifetime > 60
	Passionate	None	Lifetime > 40, Daily ≥ 50, Mood ≥ 30
	Deep Kiss	None	Love, Mood ≥ 40
Nag	About Friends	None	Mood > 40
		None	Mood ≥ 0, Nice ≥ 7
	About House	None	Mood > 40
		None	Mood ≥ 0, Nice ≥ 7
	About Money	None	Mood > 40
		None	Mood ≥ 0, Nice ≥ 7

Adult Interaction Success Requirements, continued

CATEGORY	INTERACTION	INITIATOR REQUIREMENTS	RECIPIENT REQUIREMENTS
Plead	Apologize	None	Mood > -5
		None	Lifetime ≥ 25
	Grovel	None	Mood ≥ -15
		None	Lifetime ≥ 25
Say Good-bye	Shoo	None	Daily ≤ 10
	Shake Hands	None	Daily ≥ 20
		None	Lifetime ≥ 10
	Wave	None	Daily or Lifetime ≤ 20
	Kiss Cheek	None	Daily ≥ 20
		None	Lifetime ≥ 30
	Hug	None	Daily or Lifetime ≥ 30
	Kiss Hand	None	Nice ≤ 3, Daily ≥ 60
		None	Nice ≤ 3, Lifetime ≥ 50
		None	Nice > 3, Daily or Lifetime ≥ 40
	Polite Kiss	None	Outgoing ≥ 6, Daily ≥ 40
		None	Outgoing ≥ 6, Lifetime ≥ 60
		None	Outgoing < 6, Daily or Lifetime ≥ 60
	Passionate Kiss	None	Outgoing ≥ 7, Daily ≥ 60
		None	Outgoing ≥ 7, Lifetime ≥ 65
		None	Outgoing < 7, Daily ≥ 80
		None	Outgoing < 7, Lifetime ≥ 65
Talk	About Interests	(Always Accepted)	None
	Change Subject	(Always Accepted)	None
	Gossip	None	Daily > 40
Tease	Imitate	None	Playful > 6, Mood > 50
		None	Playful > 6, Mood < 0
		None	Daily ≥ -15, Lifetime > 50, Playful ≤ 6
	Taunt	None	Mood or Daily > -20
	Raspberry	None	Mood or Daily ≥ -20, Lifetime > 25
	Scare	None	Playful ≥ 5
		None	Mood > 25
Tickle	Ribs	None	Playful > 5
		None	Mood > 50
	Extreme	None	Playful > 5
		None	Mood > 50

Adult Social Interaction Results

INTERACTION	RESPONSE	DAILY RELATIONSHIP CHANGE	LIFETIME RELATIONSHIP CHANGE	SOCIAL SCORE CHANGE
ATTACKS				
Slap	Cry	0	0	3
	Slap Back	-10	-3	-7
Be Slapped	Cry	-20	-10	-17
	Slap Back	-15	-7	3
Sissy Fight	Cry	0	0	3
	Fight Back	-8	-2	-5
Be Sissy Fought	Cry	-16	-8	-13
	Fight Back	-13	-5	3
Shove	Cry	0	0	3
	Shove Back	-8	-2	-5
Be Shoved	Cry	-16	-8	-13
	Shove Back	-13	-5	3
BRAGGING				
Brag	Good	5	0	10
	Bad	-5	0	0
Be Bragged To	Good	3	0	5
	Bad	-5	0	0
INSULTS				
Insult	Cry	-6	-3	0
	Stoic	0	-1	3
	Angry	-10	-1	5
Be Insulted	Cry	-12	-5	-10
	Stoic	-8	0	-5
	Angry	-14	-2	-7
TEASING				
Taunt	Giggle	4	0	7
	Cry	0	0	3
Be Taunted	Giggle	4	0	7
	Cry	-10	0	-7

Adult Social Interaction Results, continued

INTERACTION	RESPONSE	DAILY RELATIONSHIP CHANGE	LIFETIME RELATIONSHIP CHANGE	SOCIAL SCORE CHANGE
Imitate with Puppet	Giggle	4	0	7
	Cry	0	0	3
Be Imitated with Puppet	Giggle	4	0	7
	Cry	-10	0	-7
Scare	Laugh	5	0	10
	Angry	-5	0	0
Be Scared	Laugh	5	0	8
	Angry	-10	0	0
TICKLING				
Tickle	Laugh	8	0	10
	Refuse	-5	-1	0
Be Tickled	Laugh	5	0	10
	Refuse	-8	-2	0
Extreme Tickle	Laugh	8	0	10
	Refuse	-5	-1	0
Be Extreme Tickled	Laugh	5	0	10
	Refuse	-5	-1	0
CHEERING				
Motivate	Good	5	0	7
	Mild	0	0	5
	Bad	-3	0	0
Be Motivated	Good	10	0	10
	Mild	0	0	5
	Bad	-10	0	0
Cheer Up with Puppet	Good	5	0	7 (Sensitive: 6)
	Mild	0	0	5
	Bad	-3	0	0
Be Cheered Up with Puppet	Good	6	0	10
	Mild	0	0	5
	Bad	-10	0	0

Adult Social Interaction Results, continued

INTERACTION	RESPONSE	DAILY RELATIONSHIP CHANGE	LIFETIME RELATIONSHIP CHANGE	SOCIAL SCORE CHANGE
COMPLIMENTS				
Admire	Accept	4	1	5
	Reject	-10	-1	0
Be Admired	Accept	3	2	11
	Reject	-7	-2	0
Worship	Accept	3	1	5
	Reject	-15	-5	0
Be Worshiped	Accept	4	2	15
	Reject	-10	-4	0
DANCING				
Dance Lively	Accept	6	0	13
	Reject	-5	0	0
Be Danced with Lively	Accept	6	0	13
	Reject	-5	0	0
Dance Slow	Accept	8	2	15
	Reject	-10	-3	-4
Be Danced with Slowly	Accept	8	2	15
	Reject	-7	-2	0
ENTERTAINING				
Joke	Laugh	3	0	9
	Giggle	2	0	7
	Fail	-6	0	0
Hear Joke	Laugh	4	0	10
	Giggle	3	0	7
	Fail	-7	0	0
Juggle or Puppet	Laugh	3	0	7
	Fail	-10	0	0
Watch Juggle	Laugh	4	0	10
	Fail	-7	0	0
Watch Puppet	Laugh	4	0	13
	Fail	-7	0	0

Adult Social Interaction Results, continued

INTERACTION	RESPONSE	DAILY RELATIONSHIP CHANGE	LIFETIME RELATIONSHIP CHANGE	SOCIAL SCORE CHANGE
FLIRTATION				
Give Backrub	Accept	3	2	7
	Reject	-7	-2	0
Receive Backrub	Accept	5	3	10
	Reject	-10	-3	0
Give Suggestion	Accept	4	1	10
	Ignore	-5	0	0
	Reject	-5	-1	-10
Receive Suggestion	Accept	6	1	10
	Ignore	-3	0	0
	Reject	-7	-2	0
Check Out	Accept	5	2	10
	Ignore	-5	0	0
	Reject	-8	-1	-10
Be Checked Out	Accept	5	2	10
	Ignore	-3	0	0
	Reject	-10	-3	0
Growl	Accept	5	2	10
	Ignore	-5	0	0
	Reject	-8	-2	-10
Receive Growl	Accept	6	2	10
	Ignore	-3	0	0
	Reject	-10	-3	0
GOOD-BYES				
Shake Hand	Good	2	0	0
	Bad	-2	0	0
Have Hand Shaken	Good	2	0	0
	Bad	-2	0	0
Hug	Good	5	0	0
	Bad	-5	0	0
Be Hugged	Good	5	0	0
	Bad	-5	0	0

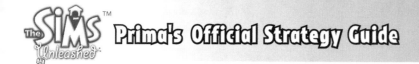

Adult Social Interaction Results, continued

INTERACTION	RESPONSE	DAILY RELATIONSHIP CHANGE	LIFETIME RELATIONSHIP CHANGE	SOCIAL SCORE CHANGE
Polite Kiss	Good	7	2	0
	Bad	-7	-3	0
Be Politely Kissed	Good	7	3	0
	Bad	-7	-2	0
Kiss Cheek	Good	3	0	0
	Bad	-3	0	0
Have Cheek Kissed	Good	3	0	0
	Bad	-3	0	0
Kiss Hand	Good	3	1	0
	Bad	-3	-3	0
Have Hand Kissed	Good	3	2	0
	Bad	-3	-2	0
Passionate Kiss	Good	10	5	0
	Bad	-10	-6	0
Be Passionately Kissed	Good	10	5	0
	Bad	-10	-6	0
Wave	Good	1	0	0
	Bad	-1	0	0
Be Waved To	Good	1	0	0
	Bad	-1	0	0
Shoo	Good	1	0	0
	Neutral	0	0	0
	Bad	0	0	0
Be Shooed	Good	1	0	0
	Neutral	0	0	0
	Bad	-3	0	0

GREETINGS

INTERACTION	RESPONSE	DAILY RELATIONSHIP CHANGE	LIFETIME RELATIONSHIP CHANGE	SOCIAL SCORE CHANGE
Wave	Good	1	0	2
	Bad	–2	0	2
Shake Hand	Good	1	0	2
	Bad	-2	-2	0

Adult Social Interaction Results, continued

INTERACTION	RESPONSE	DAILY RELATIONSHIP CHANGE	LIFETIME RELATIONSHIP CHANGE	SOCIAL SCORE CHANGE
Have Hand Shaken	Good	2	1	0
	Bad	-2	-2	0
Air Kiss	Good	2	0	3
	Bad	-4	0	-3
Be Air Kissed	Good	2	0	3
	Bad	-4	0	-3
Polite Kiss	Good	5	1	5
	Bad	-8	-2	-4
Be Politely Kissed	Good	5	5	1
	Bad	-6	-1	-3
Kiss Hand	Good	5	1	5
	Bad	-6	-2	-5
Have Hand Kissed	Good	5	1	10
	Bad	-6	-1	-3
Hug	Good	8	2	8
	Bad	-8	-2	-4
Be Hugged	Good	8	2	8
	Bad	-8	-1	-3
Romantic Kiss	Good	12	3	12
	Bad	-12	-2	-5
Be Romantically Kissed	Good	12	3	12
	Bad	-12	-2	-3

HUGS

INTERACTION	RESPONSE	DAILY RELATIONSHIP CHANGE	LIFETIME RELATIONSHIP CHANGE	SOCIAL SCORE CHANGE
Friendly Hug	Accept	4	1	8
	Tentative	2	0	5
	Refuse	-5	-1	0
Receive Friendly Hug	Accept	5	1	8
	Tentative	4	0	5
	Refuse	-5	-1	0
Body Hug	Accept	5	2	10
	Tentative	5	0	7
	Refuse	-10	-3	0

Adult Social Interaction Results, continued

INTERACTION	RESPONSE	DAILY RELATIONSHIP CHANGE	LIFETIME RELATIONSHIP CHANGE	SOCIAL SCORE CHANGE
Be Body Hugged	Accept	8	2	10
	Tentative	4	0	7
	Refuse	-10	-2	0
Romantic Hug	Accept	5	2	10
	Tentative	5	0	7
	Reject	-10	-3	0
Be Romantically Hugged	Accept	8	2	10
	Tentative	4	0	7
	Reject	-10	-2	0
Flying Hug	Accept	9	2	10
	Refuse	-15	-4	0
Receive Flying Hug	Accept	8	2	10
	Tentative	4	0	7
	Refuse	-10	-2	0

KISSES

INTERACTION	RESPONSE	DAILY RELATIONSHIP CHANGE	LIFETIME RELATIONSHIP CHANGE	SOCIAL SCORE CHANGE
Kiss Hand	Passionate	5	0	5
	Polite	4	0	4
	Deny	-5	-1	4
Have Hand Kissed	Passionate	5	0	5
	Polite	4	0	4
	Deny	-5	0	0
Kiss Polite	Passionate	6	1	7
	Polite	5	0	5
	Deny	-7	-1	4
Be Kissed Politely	Passionate	6	1	7
	Polite	5	0	5
	Deny	-6	-1	0
Kiss Tentatively	Passionate	8	2	8
	Polite	6	1	6
	Deny	-9	-2	4

Adult Social Interaction Results, continued

INTERACTION	RESPONSE	DAILY RELATIONSHIP CHANGE	LIFETIME RELATIONSHIP CHANGE	SOCIAL SCORE CHANGE
Be Kissed Tentatively	Passionate	8	2	8
	Polite	6	1	6
	Deny	-8	-2	0
Kiss Passionately	Passionate	13	4	10
	Polite	8	2	8
	Deny	-10	-3	4
Be Kissed Passionately	Passionate	13	3	10
	Polite	8	2	8
	Deny	-10	-4	0
Dip Kiss	Passionate	15	5	15
	Polite	10	2	10
	Deny	-15	-5	4
Be Dip Kissed	Passionate	15	5	15
	Polite	10	2	10
	Deny	-15	-5	0

NAGGING

INTERACTION	RESPONSE	DAILY RELATIONSHIP CHANGE	LIFETIME RELATIONSHIP CHANGE	SOCIAL SCORE CHANGE
Nag	Giggle	-1	0	3
	Cry	-4	-1	3
Be Nagged	Giggle	-3	0	4
	Cry	-8	-2	-5

PLEADING

INTERACTION	RESPONSE	DAILY RELATIONSHIP CHANGE	LIFETIME RELATIONSHIP CHANGE	SOCIAL SCORE CHANGE
Apologize	Accept	8	0	8
	Reject	-8	0	3
Be Apologized To	Accept	8	0	8
	Reject	-5	0	3
Grovel	Accept	12	0	8
	Reject	-12	0	3
Be Groveled To	Accept	12	0	8
	Reject	-5	0	3

Adult Interaction Menu Triggers

CATEGORY	INTERACTION	RELATIONSHIP REQUIREMENTS	DISPOSITION REQUIREMENTS
Ask	How Are You?	Daily > -80	Mood > -70
	How's Work?	Daily between –5 and 35, Lifetime < 40	Mood > 0
	Invite Downtown	None	At Home Only
	Invite Home	Daily > 55	Downtown Only
	Let's Hang Out/Date	None	Always Available Downtown
	Move In	Lifetime > 50, Daily > 50	Same Gender
	Propose	Daily > 75	Different Genders, In Love
	What Are You Into?	Daily between –5 and 35, Lifetime < 40	Mood > 0
Attack	Fight	Daily < -40, Lifetime < 0	Mood < 0
	Shove	Lifetime ≤ 30, Daily < -40	Mood < 0
	Slap	Lifetime ≤ 30, Daily < -40	Mood < 0
	Slapfight	Daily < -40	Playful ≥ 7, Mood < 0
Brag	Boast	None	Daily < 50, Lifetime < 40
	Flex	Daily < 50, Lifetime < 40	Body ≥ 4
	Primp	Daily < 50, Lifetime < 40	Charisma ≥ 2
Cheer Up	Comfort	Lifetime > 25, Friends	Outgoing > 3, Mood > 25, Subject's Mood < 0
		Lifetime > 5, Friends	Outgoing ≤ 3, Mood > 20, Subject's Mood < 0
	Encourage	Lifetime > 25, Friends	Charisma ≥ 2, Mood > 25
	With Puppet	Friends	Playful ≥ 6, Outgoing ≥ 4, Mood > 25, Subject's Mood < 0
Compliment	Admire	Daily between -10 and 40	Mood > 20
	Worship	Daily between -10 and 40, Lifetime between 20 and 80,	Nice > 3, Outgoing > 3 Mood > 20
Dance	Lively	Daily > 30, Lifetime > -25	Energy > 20, Mood > -20, Outgoing > 3
	Slow	Lifetime > 20	Energy > 10

Adult Interaction Menu Triggers, continued

CATEGORY	INTERACTION	RELATIONSHIP REQUIREMENTS	DISPOSITION REQUIREMENTS
Entertain	Joke	Daily > 0, Lifetime between –25 and 70	Playful ≥3, Mood > -10
	Juggle	Daily > -25, Lifetime between 0 and 70	Outgoing > 3, Playful > 4 Mood > 0
	With Puppet	Daily > -25, Lifetime between 0 and 70	Outgoing > 3, Playful > 3 Mood > 0
Flirt	Check Out	Lifetime between –10 and 10, Daily between 5 and 60	Mood > -20
	Growl	Lifetime between –10 and 10, Daily between 5 and 60	Mood > -20
	Backrub	Daily between 30 and 60, Lifetime > 30	Mood > 30
	Sweet Talk	Daily between 25 and 60, Lifetime > -50	Outgoing ≥ 7, Mood > 30
		Daily between 40 and 60, Lifetime > -50	Outgoing < 7, Mood > 30
Greet	Wave	Always Available	
	Shake Hands	Always Available	
	Air Kiss	Lifetime ≥ 5	None
	Kiss Cheek	Lifetime ≥ 20	None
	Hug	Crush	None
	Romantic Kiss	Crush	None
	Suave Kiss	Lifetime > 15	Outgoing ≥ 3
Hug	Friendly	Lifetime > 0, Daily > 15	Mood > 10
	Intimate	Lifetime > 10, Daily > 15	Mood > 20
	Leap into Arms	Daily > 40, Lifetime > 30	Mood > 25, Outgoing > 5
	Romantic	Daily > 40, Lifetime > 40	Mood > 35, Outgoing > 3
Insult	Shake Fist	Lifetime < 50	Nice ≤ 3
		None	Mood < 0
	Poke	Lifetime < 50	Nice < 3
		None	Mood ≤ 0
Kiss	Peck	Daily ≥ 20, Lifetime > 0	Mood > 0
	Polite	Daily ≥ 35, Lifetime > 15	Mood > 15
	Suave	Daily ≥ 25, Lifetime > 10	Mood > 0
	Romantic	Daily ≥ 55, Lifetime > 25	Mood > 25
	Passionate	Daily ≥ 45, Lifetime > 25	Mood > 15
	Deep Kiss	Love	Mood > 25

Adult Interaction Menu Triggers, continued

CATEGORY	INTERACTION	RELATIONSHIP REQUIREMENTS	DISPOSITION REQUIREMENTS
Nag	About Friends	Lifetime > 40	Mood ≤ -30
	About House	Lifetime > 40	Mood ≤ -30
	About Money	Lifetime > 40	Mood ≤ -3, Cash < §1,000
Plead	Apologize	Daily ≤ -10 Lifetime > 5	Mood ≤ -20
	Grovel	Daily > -20, Lifetime > 10	Mood ≤ -40
Say Good-bye	Shoo	Daily < -50	None
	Shake Hands	Daily > -50	None
	Wave	Daily > -50	None
	Kiss Cheek	Daily > -10	None
	Hug	Daily > 0	None
	Kiss Hand	Daily > 20	None
	Polite Kiss	Daily ≥ 20	None
	Passionate Kiss	Daily > 20	Outgoing ≥ 7
		Daily > 40	Outgoing < 7
Talk	About Interests	None	Available in Ongoing Conversation
	Change Subject	None	Available in Ongoing Conversation
	Gossip	None	Mood > -25
Tease	Imitate	None	Playful > 5, Mood < 15
		Daily < -20	Playful > 5, Nice < 5
	Taunt	None	Mood < 30, Nice < 5
		Daily < -20	Nice < 5
	Raspberry	None	Mood < 15, Nice < 5
		Daily < -20	Nice < 5
	Scare	None	Playful ≥ 5, Mood < 30, Nice < 5
Tickle	Ribs	Daily > 10	Playful ≥4, Nice > 4
	Extreme	Daily > 10, Lifetime between 20 and 70	Playful > 3, Nice > 4

Adult-to-Child Interactions

Adult-to-Child Interaction Success Requirements

CATEGORY	INTERACTION	RECIPIENT REQUIREMENTS
Brag		Mood > 50, Daily > 50
Cheer Up		Social ≤ 0
		Daily ≥ 0
Entertain	Joke	Playful ≥ 2
		Mood ≥ 30
	Juggle	Playful ≥ 2
		Mood ≥ 30
Hug	Nice	Mood ≥ 20
		Daily ≥ 10
	Friendly	Mood ≥ 20
		Daily ≥ 10
Insult		Daily ≥ 25
Play	Rough House	Mood ≥ 20
Scold		Mood ≥ -25
Tease	Scare	Mood between -10 and 15
	Taunt	Daily ≥ 10
Tickle		Mood ≥ 15, Playful ≥ 1

Adult-to-Child Interaction Results

INTERACTION	RESPONSE	DAILY RELATIONSHIP CHANGE	LIFETIME RELATIONSHIP CHANGE	SOCIAL SCORE CHANGE
Brag	Accept	5	0	10
	Reject	-5	-1	0
Be Bragged To	Accept	3	0	5
	Reject	-5	-1	0
Cheer Up	Accept	5	0	7
	Reject	-3	0	0
Be Cheered Up	Accept	10	2	7
	Reject	-10	-2	0

Adult-to-Child Interaction Results, continued

INTERACTION	RESPONSE	DAILY RELATIONSHIP CHANGE	LIFETIME RELATIONSHIP CHANGE	SOCIAL SCORE CHANGE
Entertain—Joke	Accept	3	1	9
	Reject	-6	0	0
Be Entertained—Joke	Accept	4	2	10
	Reject	-7	0	0
Entertain—Juggle	Accept	3	1	7
	Reject	-10	-2	0
Be Entertained—Juggle	Accept	4	2	10
	Reject	-7	-1	0
Hug—Nice	Accept	4	1	8
	Reject	-5	-1	0
Be Hugged—Nice	Accept	4	1	8
	Reject	-5	-1	0
Hug—Friendly	Accept	5	2	10
	Reject	-10	-3	0
Be Hugged—Friendly	Accept	5	2	10
	Reject	-10	-2	-2
Insult	Accept	-10	-1	5
	Reject	-6	-3	0
Be Insulted	Accept	-14	-3	-7
	Reject	-12	-5	-10
Play—Rough House	Accept	3	1	9
	Reject	-6	0	0
Be Played With—Rough House	Accept	4	2	10
	Reject	-7	0	0
Scold	Accept	5	3	5
	Reject	-8	-3	2
Be Scolded	Accept	5	3	10
	Reject	-10	-2	-2

Adult-to-Child Interaction Results, continued

INTERACTION	RESPONSE	DAILY RELATIONSHIP CHANGE	LIFETIME RELATIONSHIP CHANGE	SOCIAL SCORE CHANGE
Tease—Scare	Accept	5	1	10
	Reject	-5	-1	0
Be Teased—Scare	Accept	5	1	8
	Reject	-10	-2	0
Tease—Taunt	Accept	4	0	7
	Reject	-3	0	-3
Be Teased—Taunt	Accept	4	1	7
	Reject	-10	-1	-7
Tickle	Accept	8	1	10
	Reject	-5	-1	0
Be Tickled	Accept	5	1	10
	Reject	-8	-2	0

Adult-to-Child Interaction Menu Triggers

CATEGORY	INTERACTION	INITIATOR REQUIREMENTS	RECIPIENT REQUIREMENTS
Brag		Mood < 10, Daily ≥ 10, Daily ≤ 50	None
Cheer Up		Mood ≥ 25, Daily ≥ 25	Mood ≤ 0
Entertain	Joke	Playful ≥ 4, Mood ≥ 40	None
		Mood > 50	None
	Juggle	Playful ≥ 5, Mood ≥ 40	None
		Mood ≥ 50	None
Hug	Nice	Daily ≥ 30, Mood > 30	None
	Friendly	Daily ≥ 35, Mood > 35	None
Insult		Mood ≤ -10	None
Play	Rough House	Playful ≥ 4, Mood ≥ 20	None
		Mood ≥ 40	None
Scold		None	Mood ≤ -10

Adult-to-Child Interaction Menu Triggers, continued

CATEGORY	INTERACTION	INITIATOR REQUIREMENTS	RECIPIENT REQUIREMENTS
Tease	Scare	Mood ≤ 5	None
		Daily ≤ -5	None
	Taunt	Mood ≤ 15	None
		Daily ≤ -5	None
Tickle		Playful ≥ 2, Mood ≥ 0	None
		Mood > 30	None

Child-to-Adult Interactions

Child-to-Adult Interaction Menu Triggers

CATEGORY	INTERACTION	INITIATOR REQUIREMENTS	RECIPIENT REQUIREMENTS
Brag		Daily ≥ 10, Mood ≥ 20	None
Cheer Up		Daily ≥ 5, Mood ≥ 0	Mood ≤ 0
Entertain	Crazy Dance	None	Social ≤ 50
	Handstand	None	Social ≤ 30
	Joke	Mood ≥ 0	None
	Perform Trick	Mood ≥ 10	None
Hug	Nice	Mood ≥ 30, Daily ≥ 30	None
	Friendly	Mood ≥ 35, Daily ≥ 35	None
Insult		Mood ≥ -10, Daily ≥ -5	None
Play	Rock-Paper-Scissors	Mood ≥ 50	None
Talk	Jabber	Daily ≥ 10	None
Tease	Scare	Daily < 10, Mood ≤ -10	None
	Taunt	Daily < 15, Mood ≤ -15	None
Tickle		Mood > 5	None

Child-to-Adult Interaction Results

INTERACTION	RESPONSE	DAILY RELATIONSHIP CHANGE	LIFETIME RELATIONSHIP CHANGE	SOCIAL SCORE CHANGE
Brag	Accept	5	0	10
	Reject	-5	-1	0
Be Bragged To	Accept	3	0	5
	Reject	-5	-1	0
Cheer Up	Accept	5	0	7
	Reject	-3	0	0
Be Cheered Up	Accept	10	2	7
	Reject	-10	-2	0
Entertain—Joke	Accept	3	1	9
	Reject	-6	0	0
Be Entertained—Joke	Accept	4	2	10
	Reject	-7	0	0
Entertain—Perform Trick	Accept	3	1	7
	Reject	-5	-1	0
Be Entertained—Perform Trick	Accept	4	2	10
	Reject	-7	-1	0
Entertain—Crazy Dance	Accept	4	2	6
	Reject	-6	-1	0
Be Entertained—Crazy Dance	Accept	3	1	5
	Reject	-5	0	0
Hug—Nice	Accept	4	1	8
	Reject	-5	-1	0
Be Hugged—Nice	Accept	4	1	8
	Reject	-5	-1	0
Hug—Friendly	Accept	5	2	10
	Reject	-10	-3	0
Be Hugged—Friendly	Accept	5	2	10
	Reject	-10	-2	-2
Insult	Accept	-10	-1	5
	Reject	-6	-3	0

Child-to-Adult Interaction Results, continued

INTERACTION	RESPONSE	DAILY RELATIONSHIP CHANGE	LIFETIME RELATIONSHIP CHANGE	SOCIAL SCORE CHANGE
Be Insulted	Accept	-14	-3	-7
	Reject	-12	-5	-10
Play—Rock-Paper-Scissors	Accept	5	1	6
	Reject	-5	-1	-2
Be Played With—Rock-Paper-Scissors	Accept	7	2	6
	Reject	-9	-3	-2
Talk—Jabber	Accept	4	1	5
	Reject	-4	-2	-1
Hear Talk—Jabber	Accept	4	0	5
	Reject	-3	0	0
Tease—Scare	Accept	5	1	10
	Reject	-5	-1	0
Be Teased—Scare	Accept	5	1	8
	Reject	-10	-2	0
Tease—Taunt	Accept	4	0	7
	Reject	-3	0	-3
Be Teased—Taunt	Accept	4	1	7
	Reject	-10	-1	-7
Tickle	Accept	8	1	10
	Reject	-5	-1	0
Be Tickled	Accept	5	1	10
	Reject	-8	-2	0

Child-to-Adult Interaction Success Requirements

CATEGORY	INTERACTION	INITIATOR REQUIREMENTS	RECIPIENT REQUIREMENTS
Brag		Mood ≥ 20, Daily ≥ 10	None
Cheer Up		Mood ≥ 0, Daily ≥ 5	Mood ≤ 0
Entertain	Crazy Dance	None	Social ≤ 0
	Handstand	None	Social ≤ 0
	Joke	Mood ≥ 0	None

Child-to-Adult Interaction Menu Triggers, continued

CATEGORY	INTERACTION	INITIATOR REQUIREMENTS	RECIPIENT REQUIREMENTS
Hug	Nice	Daily ≥ 30, Mood > 30	None
	Friendly	Daily ≥ 35, Mood > 35	None
Insult		Mood ≤ -10	None
		Daily ≤ -5	None
Play	Rock-Paper-Scissors	Mood ≥ 50	None
Talk	Jabber	Daily ≥ 10	None
Tease	Scare	Mood ≤ 10	None
		Daily ≤ 10	None
	Taunt	Mood ≤ 15	None
		Daily ≤ 15	None
Tickle		Mood ≥ 5	None

Child-to-Child Interactions

Child-to-Child Interaction Success Requirements

CATEGORY	INTERACTION	RECIPIENT REQUIREMENTS
Annoy	Poke	Mood ≥ 0, Daily ≥ 15
	Push	Mood ≥ 0, Daily ≥ 10
	Kick Shin	Mood ≥ 0, Daily ≥ 5
Brag		Daily ≥ 20
Cheer Up		Daily ≥ 20
Entertain	Joke	Mood ≥ 20, Daily > -25
	Perform Trick	Mood ≥ 15, Daily ≥ -15
Hug	Nice	Mood ≥ 20, Daily ≥ 10
	Friendly	Mood ≥ 20, Daily ≥ 10
Insult		Mood > 0, Daily > 20
Play	Rock-Paper-Scissors	Mood ≥ 15
	Tag	Mood ≥ 15

Child-to-Child Interaction Success Requirements, continued

CATEGORY	INTERACTION	RECIPIENT REQUIREMENTS
Talk	Jabber	Mood ≥ 20, Social ≤ 5
	Whisper	No Data
Tease	Scare	Daily ≥ 30
	Taunt	Daily > 10
		Nice > 3
Tickle		Mood ≥ 25, Daily ≥ 30

Child-to-Child Interaction Results

INTERACTION	RESPONSE	DAILY RELATIONSHIP CHANGE	LIFETIME RELATIONSHIP CHANGE	SOCIAL SCORE CHANGE
Annoy—Push	Accept	-6	-1	6
	Reject	-6	-2	1
Be Annoyed—Push	Accept	-3	-1	6
	Reject	-7	-3	-1
Annoy—Poke	Accept	-4	0	7
	Reject	-4	-1	0
Be Annoyed—Poke	Accept	-2	0	3
	Reject	-5	-1	0
Annoy—Kick Shin	Accept	-8	-2	10
	Reject	-8	-5	2
Be Annoyed—Kick Shin	Accept	-6	-2	9
	Reject	-10	-8	-2
Brag	Accept	5	0	10
	Reject	-5	-1	0
Be Bragged To	Accept	3	0	5
	Reject	-5	-1	0
Cheer Up	Accept	5	0	7
	Reject	-3	0	0
Be Cheered Up	Accept	10	2	7
	Reject	-10	-2	0
Entertain—Joke	Accept	3	1	9
	Reject	-6	0	0

Child-to-Child Interaction Results, continued

INTERACTION	RESPONSE	DAILY RELATIONSHIP CHANGE	LIFETIME RELATIONSHIP CHANGE	SOCIAL SCORE CHANGE
Be Entertained—Joke	Accept	4	2	10
	Reject	-7	0	0
Entertain—Perform Trick	Accept	3	1	7
	Reject	-10	-2	0
Be Entertained—Perform Trick	Accept	4	2	10
	Reject	-7	-1	0
Hug—Nice	Accept	4	1	8
	Reject	-5	-1	0
Be Hugged—Nice	Accept	4	1	8
	Reject	-5	-1	0
Hug—Friendly	Accept	5	2	10
	Reject	-10	-3	0
Be Hugged—Friendly	Accept	5	2	10
	Reject	-10	-2	-2
Insult	Accept	-10	-1	5
	Reject	-6	-3	0
Be Insulted	Accept	-14	-3	-7
	Reject	-12	-5	-10
Play—Rock-Paper-Scissors	Accept	5	1	6
	Reject	-2	-1	0
Be Played With—Rock-Paper-Scissors	Accept	7	2	6
	Reject	-9	-3	-2
Play—Tag	Accept	No Data		
	Reject	No Data		
Be Played With—Tag	Accept	No Data		
	Reject	No Data		
Talk—Jabber	Accept	4	1	5
	Reject	-4	-1	-1
Hear Talk—Jabber	Accept	4	0	5
	Reject	-3	0	0
Tease—Scare	Accept	5	1	10
	Reject	-3	0	0

Child-to-Child Interaction Results, continued

INTERACTION	RESPONSE	DAILY RELATIONSHIP CHANGE	LIFETIME RELATIONSHIP CHANGE	SOCIAL SCORE CHANGE
Be Teased—Scare	Accept	5	1	8
	Reject	-10	1	0
Tease—Taunt	Accept	4	0	7
	Reject	-5	-1	-3
Be Teased—Taunt	Accept	4	1	7
	Reject	-10	2	-7
Tickle	Accept	8	1	10
	Reject	-5	-1	0
Be Tickled	Accept	5	1	10
	Reject	-8	-2	0

Child-to-Child Interaction Menu Triggers

CATEGORY	INTERACTION	INITIATOR REQUIREMENTS	RECIPIENT REQUIREMENTS
Annoy	Poke	Mood ≤ -20	None
	Push	Mood ≤ -10	None
	Kick Shin	Mood ≤ -30	None
Brag		Daily ≥ 10, Mood ≤ 20	None
Cheer Up		Mood ≥ 0	Mood ≤ 0
Entertain	Joke	Mood ≥ 25	None
	Perform Trick	Mood ≥ 25	None
Hug	Nice	Mood ≥ 30, Daily ≥ 30	None
	Friendly	Mood ≥ 35, Daily ≥ 35	None
Insult		Mood ≤ 0	None
		Daily ≤ -10	None
Play	Rock-Paper-Scissors	Mood ≥ 50, Daily ≥ 25	None
	Tag	Mood ≥ 0, Daily ≥ 30	None
Talk	Jabber	Daily ≥ 10	None
	Whisper	Mood ≥ 15, Daily ≥ 15	None
Tease	Scare	Mood ≥ 20	None
		Daily > 0	None
	Taunt	Mood ≤ 15	None
		Daily > 15	None
Tickle		Mood ≥ 5	None

The Sims Unleashed Pet Social Interaction Formulas

Key		
STR Short Term Relationship	**B**	**Recipient**
LTR Long Term Relationship	**>**	**Greater than**
A Initiator	**<**	**Less than**

> # NOTE
> *1 bar = 10 Skill points on the Pet Skills panel*

INTERACTION	AVAILABILITY	OUTCOME DETERMINATION
Adopt Stray Dog or Cat	STR with stray must be > 90. Family must have fewer than eight members, including other pets	Always good
Attack	Another Sim must be available to receive attack. Pet must have at least 30 Obedience Skill points	Always happens. Random chance for pet or attacked Sim to win
Call Over	Always	(Mood of B + STR B to A + LTR B to A + Loyal /10) / 4. Outcome is good if total is > 20, Mood > 0, and Obedience > 500
Play Tag	Mood A > 0, STR A to B > 0, B is outside	(Mood B + STR B to A + LTR B to A + Playful / 10) / 4. Outcome is good if total is > 30
Pet	Always	(Mood B + STR B to A + LTR B to A) / 3. Outcome is good if total is > 20
Give Toy: Duck	Always	(Mood B + STR B to A + LTR B to A + Playful / 10) / 4. Outcome is good if total is > 30
Give Toy: Catnip	Always	(Mood B + STR B to A + LTR B to A + Smart /10) / 4. Outcome is good if total is > 20
Give Toy: Dog Bone	Always	(Mood B + STR B to A + LTR B to A + Quiet /10) / 4. Outcome is good if total > 20
Fetch	Mood A > 25, STR A to B > 35	(Mood B + STR B to A + LTR B to A + Loyal /10) / 4. Outcome is good if total > 25
Sit and Stay	Mood of Sim > 0	Obedience skill determines result
Wrestle	Mood A > 50 or (LTR > 25 and Mood > 25)	(STR B to A + LTR B to A + Loyal /10) / 3. Outcome is good if total > 40
Put On Collar	Always	Always a good outcome, however LTR points are awarded only if LTR < 30
Hug	Mood A > 0 LTR A to B > 25	(Mood B + STR B to A + LTR B to A + Friendly /100) / 4. Outcome is good if total > 50
Train Trick	Mood A > 25 and STR B > 35	Random, but more obedient pets tend to accept more

INDEX

Children. *See also* Baby

as babysitters, 122–123

feeding, 110

Fun Motive for, 16

Hygiene of, 112

interactions table for adults and, 17–18

playtime activities for, 112–13

residence after parent's marriage of, 98

sending away, 110

training Birds, 169

walkthrough of day for family including, 109–111, 112–113

Circus career track, features of levels 1–10 of, 173–177

Cockatoos, 168–170

Comfort Motive, 14

expensive purchases as providing more, tip for, 58

items to purchase to enhance Needs state of, 59, 121

mandatory exit factors for, 15

survival tips for keeping score high for, 121

Community Lots, new, 126–143. *See also* individual areas

objects for, 187–193

Computers

buying guide for costs and Motive enhancements for, 82

tip for free use of, 36, 96

Conversations

to cultivate friendships, 30, 100

green plus sign and red minus sign for, 31

interactions and positive or negative responses to, 31–32

Cooking Skill

enhancing, 38

one expert per house required to use, 113, 116

Couches, buying guide for types, costs, and Motive enhancements for, 68–70, 179

Countertops

buying guide for costs and Motive enhancements for, 72, 179–180

placement of kitchen, 120

Creativity Skill, objects used to increase, 11, 114

Culinary career track, features of levels 1–10 of, 173–177

Custer's Market, gardening supplies from, 128–129

D

Decorative objects, buying guide for costs and Motive enhancements for, 75–79, 181–183

Depreciation of objects, table listing, 61–65

Design of house, list of considerations for, 48

Desks, buying guide for costs and Motive enhancements for, 74

Dog and cat adoption centers, 127

Dogs, 144–163. *See also* Pets and Pet Show

adopting, 145–146

attacks by, 159–160

breeding, 162–163

feeding, 137, 139, 147

housebreaking, 148, 149–150

keeping Motive levels high for, 157

napping, 147

Obedience training for, 151

raccoons fighting with, 157, 163

tricks for, 152–153

Door Tool for house building, 51, 195

E

Education career track, features of levels 1–10 of, 173–177

Electronics, buying guide for purchasing types of, 79–83

End tables, buying guide for costs and Motive enhancements for, 73–74

Energy Motive, 16

items to purchase to enhance Needs state of, 59

mandatory exit factors for, 15

survival tips for keeping score high for, 122–123

weighting of, 13

Entertainment career track

features of levels 1–10 of, 39–43

major decision for, 45

Espresso to boost Energy, 16, 134

F

Family stages of Sims, 95–103

conceiving and having baby, 98–99

married, 97–98

single, 96–97

Fashion career track, features of levels 1–10 of, 173–177